THE OUTRIDER

COLLECTED COLUMNS 2000-2006

Paul Montgomery

FEATURING: the Columbine Massacre & SCATHING REVIEWS
apologies to Elaine Sollie Herman and her photographer

AND Assorted Politicians including
Bill Clinton, Marc Racicot, George W. Bush
Dick Cheney, Jesse Jackson, Brian Schweitzer

Collection © Paul Montgomery 2012
Original columns © 2000-2006

All rights reserved. No part of this publication may be reproduced, stored in a retrieval system, or transmitted, in any form or by any means, electronic, mechanical, photocopying, recording, or otherwise, without the prior permission of Paul Montgomery or his heirs.

This book is sold subject to the condition that it shall not, by way of trade or otherwise, be lent, re-sold, hired out or otherwise circulated without the publisher's prior consent in any form of binding or cover other than that in which it is published and without a similar condition including this condition being imposed on the subsequent purchaser.

Cover photo of corner of
Brooks Street and Reserve Street in Missoula, Montana
Title page artwork,
Map of Montana
© Paul Montgomery 2012

Jacket Photo - Ellen Giamportone

ISBN 978-0-9882-0771-4

First Edition

Googolplex Publishing

For Montana

"...**R**ides ahead of the herd."

The Outrider

Collected Columns

September 11, 2000 - February 15, 2006

Table of Contents

Letter from the Editor

21

Ohs! That S'Martz!

23

O'Keefe the Change.

26

Can't We Shorten the Name?

28

Feel the Burns

30

Time-Out

33

To Berg and Rehberg

36

Keenan Wail

39

Rankin Full Stop

42

McGrath is Always Greener

44

Rice Whine

47

Brown Unbearable

49

Harp On Harper & Who Spotted J.R?

52

M-O-R-R-I-S-O-N & Schmidt's Dear

55

Terry Trieweiler Wait

57

Karla Gray Hound

60

Rowe v. State

63

Tweeten Like the Bird

66

Welcome Pat Cotter

69

Herman's Head

72

McCulloch's Chainsaw

75

All Web Picks

78

One-Month Anniversary

82

Mailbag
85

Montana and the 21st Century
86

Montana and the Republican Majority
89

Montana and the Election that Wasn't
92

Marc Racicot's Legacy
96

Mines of Desire
100

Marketing and Children
103

Bush's Anti-Democratic Tactics
106

America's Conservative Times
109

The Punditry of Marc Racicot
112

Supreme Wrangling
116

Strike it up
119

Happy Thanksgiving
122

Happy Shopping
125

Return to Denver, Part One
128

Return to Denver, Part Two
131

Return to Denver, Pt. Three
134

Return to Denver, Part Four
137

Return to Denver, Part Five
140

December in Montana
143

Blacklist...What Blacklist?
146

Do You Want Fries With That?
149

Sock It To Me?
151

Whence Cheney?
153

Going Mental
156

Here's Your Horoscope
158

Satan's Little Helper
160

Pulping Up the Volume
163

Bush and Montana
165

Patronage Primer
167

The Senseless
170

Spaced Out
172

Bork Silent, Bork Deep
174

Christmas Spectacular
176

Merry Christmas
178

Happy Returning
180

Deregulation-A-Go-Go
182
Uniformity in Action
184
There Goes the Congressperson
186
Montana's Powerless
188
Montana's Still Powerless
191
Martzomania
193
Grow Your Own
195
You Compete Me
197
Bearing the Costs
199
Stick a Pin in Me
202
Warts and All
204
Et Tu, Schneider?
206

Economic Development 101
208

Jesse and Me
210

Tooting the Horn
212

R & R Report
214

Shet Mah Mouth
216

The Raser's Edge
218

Howard's End
220

Get Lost, Marc!
222

Lincoln's Birthday
224

Big Box of Shame
226

Genuine Junk
228

Have Faith
230

Dry Me a River
233

Belated Valentine
235

Letter from the Editor
237

He Keeps Going and Going
239

Letter from the Editor
242

Letter from the Editor
244

Flipping the Flops
246

Big Brother is Eavesdropping
248

We are Martzing to Utopia
250

PSC Correct
252

Wet and Wild
254

Lies, Damn Lies, and Statistics
256

Goin' Clayzy
258

Political Postmortem
260

Punchin' Judy
263

The Get Along Gang
266

Susan Egan
268

Lynch Him!
270

Letter from the Editor
273

Gannon's to the Right of Me
275

When We Miss Her
279

Ted's Montana's Shill
282

Over 80° of Bush Google's My Party
285

Potato Nasher
289

Strange Parallels

293

Cats Carry Cary

296

Burns Misspeaks, Or Does He? Or Does He?

299

Mirror, Mirror, On the Wall, Who's the
Greatest 3-Point Shooter of Them All?

303

Montana Headline News... Brilliant Headlines

305

Montana Headline News... Headline Typos

307

Montana Headline News... Funny Headlines

308

Montana Headline News... Funny Phrases

310

Illustrations

Frontispiece
1
Montana Map
311

Letter from the Editor

Originally published September 11, 2000.

W elcome, fellow Montana lovers!

The Outrider is a magazine devoted to Montana news. This definition is broad enough to include news happening to former Montanans and trends occurring outside of the state.

Perhaps you, also, have been dissatisfied with the present media coverage in Montana. It seems too much attention is given to the surface and the sensational. I understand the need to sell dead trees and airwaves but their efforts often fail to enlighten me.

My purpose will be different. To

explore the Montana beyond the highway death count and the forecast thunderstorm.

I will achieve this by publishing the best current Montana writing and art.

Here are a few things I won't do with this site:

- You won't see any connection between the content of this site and its advertisers. I will not blur corporate public relations to turn it into news for today's content.
- I won't spend much time examining the other media. You have a limited amount of time. If you choose to view them, that is your option. We won't point out obvious deficiencies. We hope you come here for a positive alternative.
- I won't let this site degenerate into a snide view of life in Montana. The outlaws and renegades will be allowed to speak for themselves. You may bring your own attitude.
- I won't beat a dead subject or sensationalize to sell electrons.

In conclusion, let me borrow some of your precious time. I hope you will agree that The Outrider rides ahead of the herd.

Ohs! That S'Martz!

A Review

Originally published October 9, 2000.

We enter the heart of Montana political web sites for a look at the hopeful governors' web sites. Today, Judy Martz.

To begin, some stupid flashing headlines about Martz fighting for the union vote. This strikes me as a sop to her Butte roots. The infuriating part is that you are not able to click through to discover any further story. These headlines are about as deep as her appeal to working people.

In the picture of the candidates, Martz looks as though she is being goosed. Obviously, no one ever explained to Karl Ohs that a picture without the cowwear would be advisable.

And, surprise, surprise, she gains the endorsements of the living Montana Republican governors. One of the more interesting features of this home page is its stasis. I have been observing her site for over a month and the home page, the headlines, the major endorsers, have all remained wonderfully in place as though awaiting some Internet spiders to spin cobwebs across their smiling faces.

A peek into the news page reveals the latest story to be five days old. The article is self-serving puffery designed to drive home the point that Judy Martz is the true leader in comparison to her opponent's false claim to the mantel. In her own words, "This Campaign is too important for Mark O'Keefe's empty rhetoric."

Pardon me, Lieutenant Governor Martz, but this is your opportunity to display that you will provide excellent solutions and the leadership that Montana desires by providing news about issues, appearances, or plans. By engaging in the empty rhetoric you condemn and not using your Internet presence to its fullest, I'm afraid you are making a case against your organizational ability.

An excellent addition to your site would be a list of future appearances so that we could catch your act. I'll expect to see some improvement in the weeks ahead. After all, it isn't necessarily the resources you have, it is the use you put them to.

Tomorrow, Mark O'Keefe and Carol Williams get the treatment.

O'Keefe the Change.

A Review

Originally published October 10, 2000.

We continue our search of Montana political web sites with the second of the hopeful governors' web sites. Today, Mark O'Keefe.

So, this is what half a million of your own money will buy. Actually, I don't know if this is what he spent for this site, but I will say that I am holding him to a higher standard because of it.

To the site's credit the news was updated yesterday with an announcement about registering to vote. First impressions are critical and the site passes this exam. It is often updated and has the clean appearance of providing you swift passage to its interior.

The picture of the candidates is another crop job. Carol Williams has a baby head compared to Mark's prodigious melon. I believe an Internet site is important enough to have photographs taken especially for the occasion.

The O'Keefe campaign provides a secure site for a contribution but, unfortunately, provides only the barest of explanation of the use to which he will put your name and personal information. Since his site did not see fit to provide one I can sum one up thus:

You will be at the mercy of Democratic direct mailers for the rest of your natural life.

The involvement page is a good example of the clean layout of this site. Simple reminders to help surround the main choices for ways to assist. Again, there is no discernable privacy policy or way to judge how you will use my personal information should I choose to help.

This site is obviously better than Judy Martz' site. Some thought needs to be put into an O'Keefe privacy plan and his site is also missing a listing of future appearances.

Tomorrow, Brian Schweitzer faces the indignity.

Can't We Shorten the Name?

A Review

Originally published October 11, 2000.

Our seemingly never ending overview of Montana political web sites continues with the more interesting web site of Brian Schweitzer.

The quixotic character of Brian Schweitzer's campaign is wonderfully communicated by the home page of this site. If the only crime of the information age is being boring, we may all end up calling Mr. Schweitzer to post bail.

I must admit my eye was immediately drawn to the cockeyed list of links to his stands on issues. This work looks vaguely childlike. Add to that the font for Conrad Burns quote about Montanans avoiding health care and you know you are in for a great web exploration. This site just lets it all hang out design wise, as well as with content.

I have become Der Schweitzerzombie. I stumble through the day muttering, "Plain Talk...Good Ideas...Lightbulb... Brian Schweitzer."

Go ahead. I dare you to resist clicking further into this site. You have become putty. Your reluctance is overcome. You have to find out about the Do-It-Yourself Run for the Border Kit.

Please, show me ways to embarrass congress. Usually, it is the other way around.

The site does have its drawbacks. The latest news item is from June. The contribution secure site bears an unrestrained similarity to Mark O'Keefe's contribution page. However, overall the pluses outweigh the minuses.

The site is refreshing in its celebratory approach to politics. Who says running for congress has to be dull?

Tomorrow, Conrad Burns smells the glove.

Feel the Burns

A Review

Originally published October 12, 2000.

The quest to cover the wealth of Montana political web sites drags along with the mostly imperious web site of Conrad Burns.

I was unable to find a web site for Conrad Burns other than the official one that I assume he receives as a perquisite of his position as a senator. I tried to come up with reasons as to why he should have a campaign web site. The most important seemed to be these:

☯   It is a means to gather donations.

- He can update it past the 60-day deadline he states on his web site.
- Communication with constituents would be increased.

This seems like the kind of government issue web site that most senators and congressman are provided. It seems simple, functional, and as friendly as a federal building.

With Conrad Burns reputation as a supporter of all things Internet and his considerable resources as an incumbent, I must admit to my shock that he does not have a campaign web site. Does he just not care? Or, is all his effort focused on the 30-second spot on TV.

A quick comparison of the web sites of Rick Hill and Max Baucus reveals they are similarly utilitarian.

One thing about the Burns' and Baucus' sites was their being best viewed at 800 x 600. There are still some prehistoric monitors in the world which would then require scrolling. It really cheesed me off.

I thought at first that perhaps senatorial web serfs are made to create tedious web sites completely lacking in the senator's personality and designed for 800 x 600. A quick look at the web sites for Joseph Biden and Robert Byrd reveals that some senators can display a personality and not force a lowly web scribe to tax his mouse.

What more can be said of this site? It sets its sights low and it hits its mark.

Tomorrow, Dennis Rehberg feels the pinch.

Time-Out

An Experience

Originally published October 13, 2000.

The trek to discover Montana political web sites takes a well deserved break for another kind of commentary.

On this past Saturday I joined my daughter in the University of Montana Homecoming Parade. She was going to ride along with her troop of Girl Scouts.

The morning of the event dawned cold and crisp with hints of record cold seeping into my mind from the varied weather predictions I hear in the media. The parents and the Girl Scouts lined up outside of The

Oxford Bar and Cafe. The Girl Scouts' float was a trailer pulled by a pickup. The decorations consisted of hay, butcher paper, and paper plates.

As all of the groups gathered at the corner of Pine and Higgins, the University Marching Band rhythm section began to lay down a ferocious walking beat. I love a good marching band. I'm proud to say that U of M has an excellent one.

When the marching began I was completely surprised at the size of the crowd that came out for the parade. My estimate was somewhere over 5,000 people. Our part of the marching seemed to end all too quickly. I'm sure they have the Girl Scouts in the beginning section of the parade for this very reason. Don't make the little kids wait for the end of the line. The end of the line for this parade was a couple of hours away.

After ending our performance at Helen and University, we went back and watched the rest of the show. Hellgate had the best marching band of the high schools and they set down a ripping rendition of Smoke on the Water. Sentinel had the prettiest cheerleaders with Big Sky displaying the best school spirit.

The Florence marching band deserves special notice for their glorious take on Play That Funky Music, White Boy. Also, deserving of praise was the Red Wave Marching Band which was composed of musicians seemingly younger than high school age. Their act was obviously well-practiced and showed their dedication.

I was amazed at how large the parade had become. I remember some editions from the mid-1980's which lacked 90% of today's community participation and excitement. These I had only seen from a distance and I did not sense any great loss.

For me, the parade was one of the great American rituals. It imbued that Saturday with hope and pride in our young. It displayed a great Montana community at its finest.

After the parade was finished, the day brightened and warmed and became a fantastic October day.

I hope you have an excellent weekend, dear reader.

Monday, Dennis Rehberg toes the line.

To Berg and Rehberg

A Review

Originally published October 16, 2000.

The path least taken leads us to more Montana political web sites. Today, Dennis, or is it Denny, Rehberg meets his reviewer.

I have a principle that one should never attack a candidate's family photograph. These things are often uncomfortable, though largely expected by today's electorate. So, you are forced to rope your loving wife and children into posing for your campaign when it was not their idea to be related to a career politician.

I do not believe I have ever seen a really great family campaign photo and I have seen my share of bad ones. Ones that could be a real detriment. In the long term I call for a moratorium on family campaign photos. I don't think anyone will shed a tear. Plus, the family photo can remain for only the family's and friend's enjoyment.

Rehberg's web site was as hard to find as Conrad Burn's campaign site. Yes, he has one. It is called registering with Yahoo!

An interesting part of the Rehberg site is the forum page. The last posts (There were only two.) were from April. This page could probably be taken down. If the lack of interest in your site is that obvious, why advertise the fact?

This site also had a feature that I enjoyed. It was a home page button on the home page. The more I pressed it, the less it did.

In its favor the site connected to a secure site for contributions. At the same time I did not see a privacy policy. You may be hit up for Rehberg's continuing campaigns at some point in the future.

The news piece on display on the site was dated 10/11/00. That is neither especially new nor terribly old. However, I would say that pieces containing candidate quotes about the lack of integrity of their opponent do not qualify as news. "No matter how much I disagreed, at least I could always respect the old Nancy Keenan."

This site is an average effort. It managed to avoid some of the worst mistakes. Ultimately, it just does not catch any kind of creative fire or my interest.

Tuesday, Nancy Keenan ducks the book.

Keenan Wail

A Review

Originally published October 17, 2000.

More Montana political web sites await our review. Today, Nancy Keenan gets her apple polished.

"Four years ago, Montana voters told Denny loud and clear that they wouldn't stand for this sort of mudslinging and personal attacks." So says a press release on the home page of Nancy Keenan's web site. The sad part about this press release besides its obvious lame focus on the candidate's viewpoint is that it is dated October 4, 2000.

This is campaign crunch time. You

can't leave your site to stagnate for almost a week during the last month of the campaign. I would have to say this is a point to Rehberg. His news piece was equally self-referential but at least it was more current.

Speaking of news, Nancy Keenan's news page was last updated August 31, 2000. This does not provide confidence. Neither does the way her home page button fails to function.

I've spoken in these reviews of candidate's photographs. I think they say a good thousand words or better. I will add a few more in my quest for a little light.

I went off yesterday about family photos and how they could be seen as unnecessary. In Rehberg's case I believe now that they are part of a deliberate strategy. By displaying his family he purposefully shows the contrast between himself and a familyless Nancy Keenan.

Nancy Keenan fights back by including photos of her family on her web site and in her commercials. These put the argument back to Rehberg. Nancy Keenan does have a family. The photos may be old and faded but she did not come into this world alone.

The site has access to a secure site. It looks like the same one that all of the Democratic sites thus reviewed use. The Republicans did not seem so uniform. Again, the lack of privacy policy is a real detraction and could keep the camps from maximizing their web efforts.

I have to judge Dennis Rehberg the winner in this contest of the web sites. Keenan's page had a more professional appearance, however, aesthetics fail on the web where persistance and a consistent update succeed.

Wednesday, Sam Rankin does not escape.

Rankin Full Stop

A Review

Originally published October 18, 2000.

Montana political web sites seem to be reviewed forever. Today, Sam Rankin gets pulled up short.

One interesting element of the web is that it can be, for a time, a museum of the out-of-date. Such is the case with the Sam Rankin web site. Having abandoned the race for the senate to Gary Lee, his web site sits lonely and untended as a backwater of the political web site.

I must fault this site for, at least, not containing a link to any site for Gary Lee.

Perhaps, a simple link, or even a sign or crawler saying that Sam Rankin has given up his search for a political career.

Don't be surprised if Sam Rankin gets a few votes from people who have only seen his web site, been impressed with his credentials, and voted for the man not knowing that he has moved on to a less desultory future.

This site is a good example of what a person can accomplish with a limited budget. His contribution page is simply an e-mail pledge form.

One welcome part of this site is a political humor section.

Good-bye Sam Rankin, we hardly knew ye.

McGrath is Always Greener

A Review

Originally published October 19, 2000.

     Stop the insanity of more Montana Political Web Site Reviews. Today, Mike McGrath sees red.

     Besides a GIF heavy introduction (It crept up like a thief of my time.) the McGrath page has what appears to be a scanned newspaper photograph on its home page. This is a graphics sin of the highest order. Not only can you see the creases and wrinkles of the newsprint; these are transferred to the candidate, making him appear to be an older woman with a hairy double chin.

     With the latest news on his home page

being dated September 19, 2000, you know that this candidate is just not trying as hard as he could.

Taking a step back from this individual site to formulate some general impressions of electioneering and the power of the Internet it seems that the sites with the best upkeep create the best impression. Simplicity is good. Persistence is golden.

Enormous sums of money are being spent to purchase 30-second TV spots. Candidates are lashed to the fundraiser and develop bad knees from their supplicating posture. With an excellent chance to avoid intermediaries and speak directly to the voters it astonishes me to see the low level of web development of election 2000 web sites.

The web is your chance Mr. and Ms. Candidate. Use it while that precious voter is giving you a moment. Keep your site updated. Keep it simple. Banish any graphics which could detract from your race. Show off your personality. Don't be afraid to let the voters know who you are in addition to your issues.

While you are at it, don't be afraid to include large amounts of information. If someone is interested in you, allow them to fulfill their interest by providing engaging information.

Make your page compelling. Finally, make it easy for the compelled voter to donate to you. Mike McGrath's contribution page uses a service called PayPal to process donations. This service may be great, however, it is a step removed from being allowed to plop down your credit card number on a secure site and let yourself be parted from your money.

As with too many sites, this site contains no privacy policy. Also, a home button is included on the home page. This makes no sense people.

Rice Whine

A Review

Originally published October 20, 2000.

Climb every Montana Political Web Site. Review every page. Today, Jim Rice minutes.

The Jim Rice web site is little more than a kind of brochure. As such, it performs more than adequately.

The color scheme is red, white, and blue and tastefully done. The graphics load swiftly and help reinforce the message of trust, patriotism, and conservatism.

A family photograph that looks like a family photograph is placed well back on the biography page.

This site is a good example of staying simple. By avoiding contribution page dilemmas and a news page which must be kept up the candidate is able to publish a clean and hopefully effective web site.

There are negatives. There are always negatives. The home button on the home page appears again. What is the sense of this?

Yet, the site works. The candidate seems professional. Some personality shines through. How many candidates put a previous job as a "gas boy" down on their resumé? That alone earned some admiration from this reviewer.

It is one thing to set your sights low and easily obtain them. It is another to strive for simplicity and efficiency in design and achieve it while making it look easy.

Brown Unbearable

A Review

Originally published October 23, 2000.

Montana Political Web Sites haunt this reviewer. Today, Bob Brown meets his shaker.

"As Secretary of State, I'll lead the office into the increasingly technological world of the 21st Century." So says Bob Brown. This reviewer sees such sweeping rhetoric as a challenge. Viewing his ability to fly a web site as a good microcosm of his technological management abilities, this review will see if Mr. Brown can put up.

Vying for the worst campaign photograph on a candidate's home page is...the envelope please... Bob Brown. At least

Mike McGrath had the excuse that he was reproducing a news story photograph. There appears no such pretension in this instance.

One positive aspect of this site is a list of contributors updated relatively recently. Sure, it reads like a Republican roll call, but it is a step toward fuller public disclosure.

Where this site completely falls apart is after you try to contribute. Like some of the candidates he has chosen to use Rent-a-Secure-Site. In this case it is www.econtributor.net.

Before I could contribute I had to register myself. This involved giving them my personal information and then getting a user name and password. This is an unnecessary step that candidates with a better rental deal seem to avoid.

One positive that quickly turned negative was econtributor's posting of their privacy policy. This was great, but it gives you no idea of how the candidate will use your personal information once econtributor hands it over to them. In other words, it is no privacy policy at all.

The only thing worse than a site with no privacy policy is a site with a fake privacy policy.

Another infuriating moment occurred when I tried to click back to the original contribution page after looking at the registration form and the privacy policy. I eventually had to click back to the home page and reenter the contribution area. This is poor site design. Admittedly, it is probably econtributor's poor site design, but it is poor design nonetheless.

Is it just my impression or is it really bad taste to include quotes from the dead Chet Blaylock in the section of the site devoted to "What others say"? I think Chet Blaylock would probably be supporting the Democratic candidate if he were alive. I have the same inkling that Max Baucus is backing Hal Harper despite the six-year-old *Congressional Record* quotation.

<u>Special to Bob Brown - I think Max Baucus has said something nice about just about every Montanan in the Congressional Record.</u>

Add to the site's negatives the fact that it required me to scroll to see everything, the design was laughable, and his campaign graphic was sadly weak. A plus is that his Montana quiz is a great example of the writer's (I'm assuming it's Mr. Brown.) sense of humor.

The verdict. Bob Brown needs some work to become a technological leader.

Harp On Harper & Who Spotted J.R?

A Review

Originally published October 24, 2000.

Montana Political Web Sites consume my mind. Today, Hal Harper and J.R. Myers find out their zip code.

To start I have a complaint with Hal Harper's e-mail service. I sent my usual notice of review as is my custom. I received an e-mail notice of failure with the explanation that my mail service was specifically vetoed from sending mail to mcn.net. I'll have you know that I am a citizen.

When your page states that part of your vision for the office of the Secretary of State of Montana is, "Increasing access to government documents, hearings, and decisions, especially on-line," and you cannot receive an e-mail from a potential constituent you have failed in a painfully obvious manner.

The photograph on the home page is a candid shot of the candidate speaking on the telephone. This picture might be acceptable if it weren't poorly lit with over half of Mr. Harper's face in shadow.

This site is a simple one in the scheme of web sites. There is no way to contribute, volunteer, or even in my case e-mail the candidate to let him know that you could support his efforts. It is one thing to suggest that you will be an advocate for on-line voting. It is another to actually create some interactivity on your own web site.

Fortunately, Mr. Harper provides a simulacrum of community by hosting a link to a survey on the www.zoomerang.com site. He promises to let us know the results of this survey. Here's a hint, it is two weeks before the election, you may want to let us know soon.

For all of it's nice layout, the Hal Harper site is not really much greater than the simple J.R. Myers site on AOL.

Both use the web as a publishing tool for their campaign resumés and little else.

In light of Mr. Myers' and Mr. Harper's failure to capitalize on the Internet's power it

now appears that Bob Brown is a technical
leader even with all of his flaws.

M-O-R-R-I-S-O-N & Schmidt's Dear

A Review

Originally published October 25, 2000.

Montana Political Web Sites get worse and worse. Today, we go down ticket with John Morrison and Joyce Schmidt.

I noticed right away that there would be no way I could send Mr. Morrison an e-mail letting him know of this review. He has the same lazy bastard e-mail service as Hal Harper that blocks e-mail from my e-mail service. Perhaps, I could appeal to one of my readers out in Cybervania to send Mr. Morrison an e-mail at johnmorrison@mcn.net to let him know of this review.

I had a strange sense of deja vu as I was looking at this page, gif-heavy, blue background, here comes the photo of Hal

Harper. Wait, no, its John Morrison. So, the designer is guilty of recycling.

The candidate photograph is on a Batman angle. The meta-message: John Morrison is not on the level.

I have been reviewing web sites for multiple gray hairs now. I have yet to see links leading to nowhere, links that should lead somewhere but don't, and dead-end pages. This site has them all.

On Mr. Morrison's home page he has four link buttons called: background, issues, get involved, and links. Only the background and issues buttons work. When you go to the background page there are no working links and no home button. It is the roach motel of web pages. Visitors check in but they don't check out.

At least, when you go to the issues page you can still link to the background page. Is this a good thing?

This is a sloppy effort with poorly planned links, bogus buttons, confusion for visitors, no way for a helpful person to let the candidate know via e-mail where the mistakes are.

However, in the war for Montana's cyber crown showing up is half the battle and Joyce Schmidt's web site, if there is one, remains undiscovered.

Terry Trieweiler Wait

A Review

Originally published October 26, 2000.

Montana Political Web Sites ad infinitum. Today, Terry Trieweiler takes off the robe.

This site is a wonderful example of how not to design a web site. The decision to emphasize style over substance provides a poor web experience for what otherwise could be a very presentable web site.

The first mistake was to use an applet button device that produces a reasonably cool effect. My initial problem on first viewing this web site was an inability to see the cool buttons. The buttons may be cool but I was about to give up, when upon my return to the site the buttons were active and in place. How many people give up before I did?

These buttons caused the site to load slowly on every page. This was simply unacceptable for an effect which ended up being far more annoying than enjoyable.

Another problem I had with the site was the gray background. Rather, I should say the designer had a problem with the gray background. When they created white titles in front of the gray, they were practically invisible. This was most pronounced on the biography page.

Add to the design problems some of the bizarre ways to list data. Again, refer to the biography page. This looked like it was taken from a questionnaire or was written by a person with English as a second language. I have no idea why someone would produce biographical information in this manner.

Take a gander at the endorsements page for more of this weirdness. Under the first endorsement is the phrase, "Cite support for working families and openness." This almost seems like a note to the web designer more than something which should be included on the final product.

This brings me back to cool buttons. They were built with little foresight and some of the headings are too wide for the buttons and this causes the letters to be chopped off.

How can I let his picture go uncommented upon? This picture seems like a campaign photograph and the quality of the picture is high. It is well lit and the colors are good. Now, if you could only get the candidate to not appear so smug and full of himself.

In the site's favor is its coverage of past supreme court verdicts Trieweiler had a hand in. This kind of information is perfect for deciding a vote for chief justice.

The only problem is the crap. Get rid of the crap and Mr. Trieweiler would have a good site.

Karla Gray Hound

A Review

Originally published October 27, 2000.

Montana Political Web Sites join at the horizon. Today, Karla Gray bangs the gavel.

Karla Gray and Terry Trieweiler have to have the best campaign photographs of any candidates. Ms. Gray decided to go with the black-robed look. I feel kind of guilty saying that Ms. Gray cuts a comely figure. One shouldn't make such comments of a judge.

This site is basic and I'm battling boredom to try to provide you with something witty or interesting. The buttons mostly worked. Look at the court decisions links page. The news links don't work.

I'm fighting back the tears of sleep to render this page for those of you without taste or talent enough to make up your own mind about a web site. I hope you appreciate my efforts.

Hey, here's an interesting item I discovered about this page. The volunteer and contribute pages are the same.

I'm sorry. I dozed off for a while there. Another technique which I don't think worth copying is the graphic of a newspaper page for Ms. Gray's news section.

I think it must be getting time for me to go to bed. I am battling back the yawns for you, dear reader.

This is the type of site that does not achieve much. I don't think there is much here to rouse a supporter or to anger a critic.

I don't feel like I know any more about Karla Gray after looking at this page. Other than I should be caffeinated in her presence.

In marathon running they speak of

hitting the wall. Karla Gray is my wall and I am hitting her. I am laughing giddily as I type this.

    There, I did it. I actually squeezed some blood out of this turnip of a web site.

Rowe v. State

A Review

Originally published October 30, 2000.

We can't help ourselves and continue to peruse Montana Political Web Sites. Today, Bob Rowe and the rest of the PSC gang.

In the weeks of reviewing web sites I have kept a wary eye peeled for typos and errors in English. To my amazement there has been little to report. The sites have displayed a remarkable level of editing and proofreading. I cannot say the same for the Bob Rowe web site.

"What the PSC does affect your pocketbook and the quality of your life, now and for years to come." This is on the home page and it is one of several glaring misspellings. Bob Rowe would have done well to have someone help with the editing of his site. If he did get help, he should get his money back.

His re-election announcement is a particularly grievous example of his mistakes. There is no need to go into their enumeration. I will leave that up to the individual reader.

How about the picture of Bob Rowe on the home page? Would you buy a previously-owned snowmobile from this man?

One source of pleasure for this reviewer was the picture of Bob Rowe in front of a banner declaring "High Speed Internet" on his biography page. This graphic loaded at a soul-suckingly slow rate. When it finished the quality was awful.

A simple feature, which I appreciated, was the printable contribution page. This was a nice touch and an easy way for a supporter to provide a donation.

It is probably a good indication of the lackluster attention shown toward the PSC races that Bob Rowe is the only candidate in any race who even has a web site. And bless his soul, he has no competition. He is providing a window into the PSC and its workings in spite of the apathy displayed by the other candidates.

In these days of upward trending energy prices and the uncertain effects of deregulation, it would seem that the races for PSC would be higher profile. We have only to look in the mirror dear voter. Our languishment will cost us.

The PSC is not blameless though. Their attitude of submission in the wave of mergers and corporate asset sales sets the tone for Montana's pathos. I read of other western states that force corporations to provide monetary settlements due to poor service prior to approving mergers. I also read of payments made by corporations to the public treasury as they sell their public-supported monopolistic energy generating facilities. It is Montana's lot to remain pathetic only as long as it accepts failure in its public servants and their record of service.

I wish more candidates for the PSC had felt obliged to provide web sites to inform voters. As it is, we grope forward in the dark.

Tomorrow, we tweek Chris Tweeten.

Tweeten Like the Bird

A Review

Originally published October 31, 2000.

Stop us before we review Montana Political Web Sites, again. Today, Chris Tweeten sings like a canary.

Chris Tweeten's picture seems to slyly suggest, "I'm kinda dopey." The color scheme is yellow and black and lacks all subtlety.

The home page, which loads after a cheesy splash false home page, has what wins the prize for the largest paragraph on a candidate page. Break things up a bit.

I had to scroll back and forth on every page of the site. Do I need to mention I find that annoying?

Then, on the bottom of the page I see that the page was designed by Mr. Tweeten's son Andy. This is neither a source of derision nor of pity. I am giving this site a straight review in line with all of the other site reviews I have previously endured.

One small and admirable feature of the site was the inclusion of Mr. Tweeten's phone and fax number. This is the kind of openness that Montana cherishes.

A basic list of news items and press releases has its most recent article dated October 12. This is a bit better than most.

Another annoyance was the number of errant spaces appearing on the sample letter to the editor page. Can we blame these on Microsoft? I think the culprit has the initials A.T.

For pleasure seekers, you can't beat the photos page where Mr. Tweeten obviously ignored the pundit wisdom of never wearing a hat as a candidate. This resembles nothing so much as a family album.

There is little on this page to provide a source for the voting decision. Maybe some copies of work produced for the attorney general. As innocuous as such documents would be, they are missing.

This site does not provoke much in the

way of positive reaction. His family looks kooky and fun. So, they've got that going for them.

As sites go, this is a basic effort and not a terribly good one at that.

Tomorrow, we take the blotter to Pat Cotter.

Welcome Pat Cotter

A Review

Originally published November 1, 2000.

Don't blame us if we review more Montana Political Web Sites. Today, Pat Cotter pins her hopes.

The photograph of Pat Cotter on this web site reminded me of Betty Crocker. Only not so cool. Really, the pearls and too conservative attire took me aback.

This web site has an appealing design in its favor. The gray background is not disturbed by the state seal or the office seal as has been seen on a few web sites. It remains calm and soothing. There are no blinking animations to disturb the atmosphere.

This site did have the best and most obvious typo thus discovered. It is for the button that should be labeled "endorsements". The humorous part is that the little pop-up tag seen by hovering the mouse is actually spelled correctly.

Aw, who am I kidding? This site is as dull as either Karla Gray's or Chris Tweeten's.

There is very little to go on for a voting decision. I suppose that is why the judicial candidates seem to rely on their endorsement pages to be a stand-in for declaration of party affiliation. The AFL-CIO is for Pat Cotter and the Chamber of Commerce is for Chris Tweeten.

I doubt that either candidate is so hardened to an idealogy. Perhaps, the endorsing organizations may come to regret their endorsements. Besides, I wonder how the organizations come to know who to support.

There is something distasteful in imagining justice candidates conveying with a wink and a nudge that they are a friend to labor or business. Perhaps, we are trying to avoid a greater evil of judicial hopefuls declaring a party preference. Maybe we need to accept that a judge will probably have an idealogy.

Besides, many of the issues ruled upon by courts do not cut along the same lines as most political issues. For some reason political conservatives seem to favor a more generally restrictive legal society even as they celebrate free markets. Liberals tend to favor personal freedom all the while proposing governmental solutions.

Does a Democratic or Republican label help me to make a decision about which justice to cast my vote for? There are too many intervening factors.

In addition, the strange cultural restrictions binding justices leads to them being our own secular priesthood. Have you ever had a drink with a judge? Seen a judge at a bar? Shared a laugh with a judge?

Somehow, I think these people must have a life. I have never seen the evidence of the same but they must. The troubling part is...do you want someone who doesn't really live to rule about your own messy and sybaritic life?

Herman's Head

A Review

Originally published November 2, 2000.

Why more Montana Political Web Sites? Today, Elaine Sollie Herman lines 'em up.

Want to see something really scary? Look at Elaine Sollie Herman's photograph. Halloween is not over. It continues.

The lighting, the makeup, the attire, the smile; all of these conspire to create something truly terrifying. I shudder to think that she had this picture taken strictly for her campaign.

The fun part of reviewing superintendent candidate's web sites is that I have the opportunity to grade the graders. With education as their goal I pledge to show no mercy in my appraisal. After all, an honest review will only help them to improve.

There is no way to review Ms. Herman's site without at least referencing her comment about shooting troublemaking students. This remark bought her some front page space in the *Wall Street Journal*. The callous jest, while identifying some extreme parental frustration, has irretrievably tainted Ms. Herman's campaign and now colors all of her actions including her web site.

Can I avoid mentioning that she is endorsed by the Montana Shooting Sports Association and the National Rifle Association? Oops, I guess it slipped out. This is obviously a matter of pride for Ms. Herman. These are two of the first three endorsements listed for Ms. Herman and appear at the top of her page.

How important is it for an educator to be endorsed by the gun lobby? Two out of three gun manufacturers recommend our candidate for school superintendent. This could send the wrong message to children.

How will this teach kids, in the words of the blues song, "If you don't play with guns, guns won't play with you." There may be a few organizations disgraceful enough to avoid taking money from. The National Rifle Association may be one for school superintendents.

Ms. Herman hails from my old hometown of Broadview. I want so badly to say that she has her act together but I only need to provide some quotes to show where Ms. Herman's head is at. How about, "I not only know I can WIN, I know I MUST win!

"Please help me if you want the educational system to understand who works for whom (the parents are the customers), if you want to see fiscal responsibility in education, and if you want students taught skills and knowledge, not intrusive social matter which interferes with family values."

How about this little monologue with Elaine talking to Elaine? "Bring HOPE to our schools with......CASH!... Lots of it!

"This campaign is costly, but not as costly as electing another 'educrat' who sees money as the answer to every problem which come down the line. It's not too late to bring back old-fashioned values and common sense to our schools."

I hope she's worked this problem out by our next visit. We'll leave her alone now.

McCulloch's Chainsaw

A Review

Originally published November 3, 2000.

Is this the last Montana Political Web Site? Today, Linda McCulloch gets sent back.

Linda McCulloch has the fuzziest picture of any candidate I have seen. Was she even in the frame? I couldn't tell.

Her picture is one of the clearest things on this confusing and poorly executed web site. It is even less broken up and distorted than her logo.

Right off the bat, I am confessing that I am giving Linda McCulloch an incomplete. She needs to present a higher level of work.

The page has an apple theme. This apple is as sloppy as the logo. This is because it looks like it was cut and pasted from the logo. The apples go together with the ruled lines of what appears to be notebook paper as a background. This background was more confusing than helpful and it did not seem to stop the designer from using a great variety of sizes of fonts in several locations and contexts.

Her biography is a layout nightmare. Particular discredit is due to the public service column. This was impenetrable. I did not even attempt to read it.

One of her quotes in her job history was, "Riffed due to school closures." This marks her as a career bureaucrat. If you, dear reader, have not had the misfortune to be exposed to bureaucracy in its most contagious form, you may not know what "riffed" means. It is the past tense of the acronym RIF which stands for Reduction In Force. This is public service mumbo jumbo for laid-off or fired. You would use it in the conversation, "I've been riffed. Have you?"

Ms. McCulloch does get credit for being able to edit. Her volunteer is brevity itself. And, it is one of the few well designed pages.

Her candidate's letter page is the worst form of self-serving tripe. Say, maybe I'll copy that idea. I can invite the president to view the world's greatest web site.

This page is also infamous for having only one of her link buttons functional. The functional button goes to a list of related sites. It's almost as if she is saying, "Here, go to a well produced page."

I saved the worst for last folks. Yes, it is the page for news clips. This takes the cake in the saddest layout contest. A graphic obscures text. The layout is squashed against the side in what looks like a painful position for all those electrons.

This web site is plain pathetic. If it was handed in as homework it would have to be redone.

It is so hard judging web sites. Who is worse, Ms. Herman and her typos or Ms. McCulloch and her poor design?

Come back Monday for *The Outrider's* all web picks.

All Web Picks

A Review

Originally published November 6, 2000.

        It is finally over. Every statewide candidate for elective office who produced a web site has been reviewed. Let me state from the start that the level of work was generally judged to be pathetic.

There was very little attempt at interactivity. The sites rarely contained privacy policies. Updating the web sites did not appear to be a priority of the campaigns. Layout and design were either overdone or underdone more often than done right.

The quality of the candidate photographs was low. Poor lighting, bad poses, inexplicable dress, and an unforgivable use of general purpose photos in place of a specific campaign photograph were among the abuses.

One consolation would be that a motivated voter would have a difficult time finding these sad sites. The level of registration to web directories was an embarassment. How can voters find your site if they cannot find it via a web directory?

All of these factors taken into consideration we present *The Outrider*'s all web picks. These choices are based solely on the candidate's web site and not on their positions.

Mark O'Keefe for governor. This site was so far ahead of Judy Martz's site that there was not much to consider. At this level of race it is necessary to have a contribution page that allows a voter to donate on-line.

Brian Schweitzer for senator. Conrad Burns showed some cyber ignorance by not registering his site. I missed it the first-time around. Brian Schweitzer lets his personality shine in what is a dull morass of web sites.

Dennis Rehberg for representative. How can Nancy Keenan expect to compete when she leaves her site to stagnate for a month before the election? Her last press release is dated October 4th. Dennis Rehberg has put in the time to update his web site and it shows. His last posting on his home page is dated October 29th.

Persistence works.

Mike McGrath for attorney general. Jim Rice had the best design and layout of any site reviewed. His downfall came in not updating the site and in not providing a way to contribute on-line. Mike McGrath still has that terrible newspaper photograph on his home page.

Bob Brown for secretary of state. Again, it comes down to having a way for citizens to contribute on-line. Hal Harper and J. R. Myers gave us brochure sites without contribution pages.

John Morrison for state auditor. Joyce Schmidt is AWOL. In a sign of his responsiveness, John Morrison has left the broken links on his page.

Terry Trieweiler for chief justice. This was a close one. The deciding factor was the court opinions page of Mr. Trieweiler. A voter could use this information to make decision. Karla Gray's court decisions page was just a bunch of links and not terribly helpful.

Bob Rowe for PSC. He wins by default as no one else competed.

Pat Cotter for justice. She won on points primarily for design. Chris Tweeten relied on his son to build his site and it showed.

Linda McCulloch for superintendent of

schools. This was a choice of the least worst site. I was shocked and disgusted to see the low level of quality on the sites of our choices for top school officer. Neither of these women can take pride in their work. Elaine Sollie Herman's typos rated worse than Ms. McCulloch's layout errors.

One-Month Anniversary

An Experience
Originally published November 7, 2000.

I am not much of a person for celebrating anniversaries. Election day 2000 was as good of an excuse as any to take a moment to express myself.

What started as an unfulfilled desire has been made real. I needed *The Outrider* as much as you, dear reader. A forum for the unspoken, the undisclosed, and the undesired has been created.

In the weeks and months ahead look for *The Outrider* to expand its voices. As always, I welcome your expressions.

The level of interest has been incredible. I am astonished and wonderfully surprised every day by your responses.

You may look forward, as well, to see news being broken by *The Outrider*. In the wake of the election, web site reviews will give way to a wider and more varied content.

I must admit to being a little scared seeing the first response to a web site review. It is frightening to put yourself in front of the public as a self-appointed expert. Luckily, the letter writer thanked me for the review and gave me the benefit of their opinion. Almost everyone who wrote in included their thanks, even when their review was difficult or harsh.

Speaking of letters, I still haven't received an answer from Conrad Burns other than his form e-mail about three weeks ago. Well, I hope he is hard at work, rather than answering my silly epistles.

I feel I have gained a great education about the candidates. I am going to have a tough time pulling the lever for either likely school superintendent. Such patent disregard for the language is not reassuring.

On the other hand some races have defied expectation to produce choices between extremely well qualified contenders. The contests for secretary of state, attorney general, and the two justices are very close. Could their web sites make a difference? I would like to think so.

The Internet is an alluring media. It

allows you to attract your audience. The primary focus for marketing in the pre-digital era was to push your product to a mass audience or to a niche of that mass.

Now, you are able to create a personal, eccentric product and attract an audience interested in that specific item. The market selects itself.

Thank you, for your time. We continue the journey together.

Readers dip their quills.

Mailbag

We may print your letter, too.

Originally published November 7, 2000.

Karla Gray Rules in our Favor

Paul,

With apologies for the delay in responding, I did see the outrider on Trieweiler's web site. Did you see it on mine? It was about as favorable--but a hoot, in some ways, since I'm described as "comely" as opposed to "smug" for my opponent.

Karla

Montana and the 21st Century

An Opinion
Originally published November 8, 2000.

For most of the first 100 years of Montana's statehood Montana was a company state. The Anaconda Company held sway over our economy, our environment, and our government.

With Anaconda's demise in the early 1980's Montana faced a decade of uncertainty. During the '80's Montana's transition from a one-company state provoked difficulties across our entire society. If we were no longer Anaconda's state, who were we?

Add to these problems a general drop in commodity prices, the continued out-migration of our promising youth, and a national economy providing prosperity on the coasts but not in the heartland. The 1980's were not for the weak or infirm. Montana weeded itself of the wishy-washy.

The 1990's have been incredibly different. The economy stabilized. It grew, maybe not as much as nationally, but this smoothed over many of the '80's hurts. Commodities stabilized. The lack of inflation allowed for expansion. The migration tide turned and more people were seeking to come to Montana than to leave.

As the year 2000 packs its bags and prepares to go it is appropriate that Montana Power, Anaconda's twin, will leave with it. This will leave Montana without a corporate vestige of Anaconda. I know that Arco and Asarco remain but they were never the paternal influence either of the twins were.

Rather than looking backwards and lamenting our corporate heritage, I think this is a great opportunity to look forward and embrace a future without a dominant corporation. Knowing the lessons of corprocracy we are in a unique situation to never again repeat the past.

What are the lessons of the Anaconda-Montana Power years?

As much as our founding fathers distrusted government, we must never again place such unbridled trust in any corporation. Corporations have at least as much possibility to become as overweeningly bullying as any man.

Our Montana market must become diversified. Reliance on a single company, as well as a single commodity became a copper collar when prices did not hold or the company wanted to force our economic compliance.

There is strength in numbers. The companies kept wages depressed for their benefit. They discouraged additional investment in the state. A low-population state suited their purposes. The gains Montanans made came through joining together as with the 1972 constitution. When our population increased as in the 1990's we enjoyed a burgeoning economy.

I am sure there are more. Perhaps, they will become clearer as we proceed into our third decade without Anaconda and our first without Montana Power.

One thing is certain. Montana will now be standing on its own for the first time in its history.

Montana and the Republican Majority

An Opinion
Originally published November 9, 2000.

The election results are in and one thing is clear. That Montana is a solidly Republican state in several different ways.

Montana joins with most of the West in going Republican in every presidential election. By West, I don't mean the West coast which seems as reliably liberal. We are not the safest of states for the Republicans like Idaho or Wyoming but we are dependable.

I am still unsure of the reason for this. I tend to think that it is psychographics more than anything. Westerners seem to identify with the supposed toughness of the Republican candidate. With Democrats there lingers a compassion at odds with the harsh realities of Western living. This explanation is most satisfactory to me since most often Western issues are ignored.

With the power of personality and some relationship between Republicans and machismo, Montanans vote for the GOP at the national level. The economy explains the Republican hold at the state level.

Despite a desperate try to sell the state as an economic badland, the Democrats failed to revoke the prosperous good times. After all, everything is relative, and in Montana the economy has been good for most of the 1990's. Sure, we have not had the gains of other states but things are by no means lamentable.

In the path of the 1980's poor economy, Montana increasingly turned to the Republicans. As the 1990's prospered, the GOP has reaped the gains. A feel-good governor has enjoyed the glory and passed that on to his successor.

Martz, Rehberg, and Burns are all the beneficiaries of this gratitude from Montana voters. These races especially were gained from economic well-being.

The other statewide races were won by the personality and effort of the candidates involved. These were not as affected by the economy.

Often, with the down-ticket races it

hinges on name recognition. Bob Brown, Mike McGrath, and John Morrison all counted on this element to propel them to victory and it did. I propose that they probably would have won a name recognition poll by the same margin at the beginning of this contest.

Sometimes it is just enough to hope your opponent does not show up. Or, conversely, or, perversely, to wait for her to shoot the foot in her mouth. Such was the case with Linda McCulloch and Elaine Sollie Herman.

So, for the four statewide offices below the governor's office, the Democrats won three. This was the result of good candidate recruitment on their part along with the other factors cited above.

Montana is a committed Republican state except where likeability and a good name intervene.

Montana and the Election that Wasn't

A Phantasy
Originally published November 10, 2000.

The Manipulated Press has projected Gore the winner of the Oregon balloting. With 267 electoral votes Al Gore only needs one small 3-vote state in his column to win. Disturbing reports from Montana suggest that it may have gone for Al Gore in a big way. Widespread allegations of voter fraud are rocking the treasure state.

Entire boxes of ballot from the liberal city of Billings have apparently been misplaced and in some cases lost entirely. Voting chair of Yellowstone County states, "It might have been the rock chucks. Many of these polling places were in the rural areas."

Meanwhile, the more conservative city of Butte seemed to have found a way to raise enough Republican voters from the cemetery to have given Bush the edge. This, plus apparently any recently deceased Butte voter's decision to vote for Judy Martz pushed the Republicans to victory.

But there are far more disturbing items of interest as *The Outrider* has learned of an impending influx of unfriendly Northerners. No, it is not the cast of *Montana Live*. Turns out it could be the Canadians.

With Marc Racicot as the cat's-paw of the Albertan provincial government and especially it's leader Jean Poutine, the United States is ripe for a takeover from above. In other news, Brian Schweitzer is rumored to be appointed to the Internation Border Herbicide Committee by President Clinton. This group while pretending to kill the weeds along the border is actually preparing the way for this invasion of United Nations' troops disguised as Canadian mounties on holiday.

Mark O'Keefe invested in training depots even as he slyly masqueraded as a candidate for governor. By acting as Judy Martz's shill he was able to subtly brainwash Montanans into experiencing their worst nightmare. By being in cahoots with business interests he was able to provide himself cover for bankrolling the coup.

Meanwhile, the two secret stealth agents of the Maple-traitors, Dennis Rehberg and Conrad Burns, will return to Washington to weaken the nation by usurping the people's rights to Aunt Jemima syrup, a perfectly acceptable and buttery-tasting substitute for tree sap. With this done, both men will have accomplished their main goal of leaving Montana to the mercy of the puck-people.

Some state leaders have already called for calm during the impending crisis. Elaine Sollie Herman has stepped to the fore as a peacemaker. She has pledged to line the Canadians across the border in a celebration of humanity known as "Germs Exchanged Freely".

In other shocking developments, state somethingorother candidate Joyce Schmidt has revealed that she may or may not be a man. We wish her well.

With ballot measures in Montana to create an account of accounts winning a substantial majority, citizens are still scratching their heads. Maybe, this confusion is part of the plot.

Anyway, the nation holds its breath while Montana decides the next president. Voters in East Missoula are claiming that it was kind of windy and chilly that day preventing a full tallying of the results. One confused resident even appeared to sober up as a result of the attention.

We promise to stay vertical on this story while it remains in the open. Look here for full developments. Remember, it is important to keep your sense of humour in these times.

Marc Racicot's Legacy

An Opinion
Originally published November 13, 2000.

Time to cast a backward glance at the accomplishments of the man who might be Montana's most popular governor in history. This list will be neither exhaustive nor particularly detailed, but based on my reminiscence.

There were whispers when Marc Racicot ran for governor that he was a closet Democrat. In fact, I remember telling a joke in which I asked who was the Democrat. Dorothy Bradley, his first opponent, is a conservative Democrat.

The outcome of that race was tremendously close. In a sign of the times, the issues of 1992 skewed to the more liberal. Racicot would face continuing opposition from the right wing of his own party over positions advocated and then forgotten. One of them was increased access to health care.

The main area of agreement for both candidates was the need for a sales tax. With Racicot's election he did try to enact a sales tax. The citizens of Montana can thank Rob Natelson for leading a vigorous opposition to all the taxing efforts of the new governor. From that point on Rob Natelson became Racicot's antagonist. Racicot's sales tax proposal was rejected by more than a majority of Montanans. It would prove to be the last major proposal of Marc Racicot.

I have always been struck by the similarities between Marc Racicot and Bill Clinton. Their rhetoric was similar in 1992. Both regarded healthcare as a major priority. Both lead half-hearted and weak efforts to enact healthcare proposals and both abandoned them quickly. Rob Natelson is scorned for making this point but I agree with the man. Marc Racicot sounded in favor of activist government at the time. So did Clinton.

Both Racicot and Clinton became tremendously popular for leading during positive economic times. Both faced weak, elderly opponents in their 1996 elections. Rob Natelson did provide a challenge in the primary but was soundly defeated.

One aspect to Racicot's personality is distinctly similar to Clinton's and another is sharply differing. Racicot relies on positive rhetoric to appease critics and pacify activists. Like Clinton, he dispenses abundant sunshine. Unlike Clinton, he has been all too willing to seek a legal avenue of redress as a first effort of settlement. Racicot turns to the courts without seeking a negotiated outcome.

These twin effects have been most pronounced with regard to the Yellowstone buffalo. His cheery announcements continue year after year. He ties up the government in court. The ill results remain.

By 1994, he rediscovered his Republicanism by suggesting a tax refund. This was immediately popular but remarkably was never repeated. In the wake of the tax refund Republicans won both houses of Montana's legislature and haven't looked back.

Perhaps, Marc Racicot's most shameful legacy will be the terrible contract administration for the mental health managed care plan. There were no safeguards to prevent the contractor from selling itself and its contract to a higher bidder. After a couple takeovers the contract had to be cancelled due to widespread complaints.

From a candidate promising greater access to health care to a governor doling out health care to the members of society least able to challenge a sinking program, Marc Racicot had come a long way on the road of political expediency.

Problems with buffalo from the beginning of Mr. Racicot's term are still with us. His charming lyrics and his love of the courtroom have kept this problem from resolution.

Whither Racicot? So much depends on his benefactor's success. Judging by his desire to please and his obvious ambition Marc Racicot will probably continue in politics. With a national audience, however, Marc Racicot might become the same sort of partisan lightning rod as Bill Clinton.

Mines of Desire

A Review
Originally published November 14, 2000.

       I had the good fortune to watch an exceptional television program this Sunday. It was called *Butte Symphony Orchestra: 50th Anniversary Concert: A Look Inside*. It aired on Montana PBS at 3:30 pm. They ran it in September, also. If you get a chance, you must watch the program.

       The main focus of the program was a commissioned piece of music written especially for the Butte Symphony by Erik Santos. I am unsure of the spelling. The show was roughly split into three segments. The first was an explanation of the music. The second was the performance itself and the third was the Symphony in C (organ) by Camille Saint-Saëns.

The name of the composition was *In the Mines of Desire*. The conductor for the evening was Matthew Savery. Conversations between Mr. Savery and Mr. Santos were intercut with Mr. Savery's explanation of the evening's entertainment.

Mr. Savery and Mr. Santos spoke of having worked together previously. They obviously had great regard for each other. Mr. Santos related having composed certain sections keeping in mind Mr. Savery's physical presence as a conductor.

The intercutting was an effective technique. It allowed what might have been a dull introduction to turn into a fine interplay between artistic comrades. The didactic quality was blunted by Mr. Savery's and Mr. Santos' evident delight.

Forgive me if I mix up movements. I made notes as best I could and I was swept up in the music at points so I did no writing. I would also add the caveat that I am no music afficionado. I just know what I like and this musical opus won my heart.

A little about the television production itself. It was produced by Aaron D. Pruitt and directed by Jack Hyyppa. The production seemed extensive. I had the feeling of multiple cameras and numerous angles. Mr. Hyyppa's direction enhanced the experience of the viewer. At one point their was a harp section. This was captured with an overhead shot that provided an angelic sensibility to this viewer. In another's hands this camera angle may have been overplayed but the director stayed just long enough to accentuate the strings' heavenward plaint.

A haunting chorus commenced the 1st movement. This represented the potential of the mountains even before the first people arrived.

The 2nd had excellent use of percussion. This stood for the activity surrounding Butte and its beginnings.

With the 3rd came the bacchanal feast of percussion stark and staggering in its power. This was something akin to both a war dance and a Roman march.

Near the end, *Rock of Ages* was sung with haunting, droning overtones enveloping the chorus.

"Rock of Ages cleft for me, Let me hide myself in thee"

I can never remember whether that is hide or find. Either way, it seemed to paint a portrait of Butte.

It was revelatory and transforming. I can't remember when I felt so moved by a musical performance. I had to write about it, even if I have not done it justice.

Marketing and Children

An Experience
Originally published November 15, 2000.

As parents asked for cookie orders at many of my workplaces, I smugly thought that I would never be in their position. I would never stoop so low as to ask coworkers for mere cookie orders.

Aha! Time and circumstances capture us all and, yes, I asked for nut orders from my fellows to raise money for my daughter's Girl Scout troop. I had joined that bastion of multi-level children's marketing.

The Girl Scouts continually win praise for their coordinated fund-raising efforts. They are one of the best groups in the country in terms of their strategy and execution of resource gathering. This is all good. I felt like I had become a cog in the machinery of Girl Scouts, Inc.

I realize that if the various troops were to hold their own events to raise money that some would be pathetic and raise no money at all. That having a national brand and the name recognition it accompanies helps many a lesser troop meet its needs for the year. Again, this is all to the good. I still feel like it has traded personality and drive for efficiency and consistency.

I love to raise money and being handed the packet to sell nuts was a wonderful challenge. I went forth dutifully and within a day I sold a solid amount of nuts and magazines. My daughter did not need to be concerned with selling these products. After all, she is only six and the deadline for sales loomed. There was just no time to have her ask enough people.

This, combined with being relatively new in town, lead me to the conclusion that the workplace was the logical choice. And, indeed, it proved to be.

It amazes me how humbling parenting proves to be. Look at the parents, you singles. You laugh now. They appear funny. Maybe they look tired. Maybe depressed. Time will provide you with sympathy.

Another experience similar to the first occurred at my daughter's school. I was there for the parent-teacher conference. While I was there they held a book sale to raise money for the Parent Teacher Association.

Of course, I admired their willingness to take advantage of the opportunity. Every parent was passing through the school at this time. Why not hit them up for some money through a book sale? Then, parents can give the books for Christmas.

The thought of using a school and parent-teacher conference time for fund-raising is still a tad unsettling to me. Isn't the purpose of a school and a conference, the education of our children, not the selling of our children?

But, thinking about it some more, haven't schoolhouses always been about community in their own way. I am sure there have been innumerable fund-raisers in schools across the country for many worthy aims. Money does not always flow to the areas we value and needs to be redirected at times. When this task is taken on by the people, isn't that the definition of public spirit?

Oh well, I am sure that the parents selling books I look askance at now, will one day be me. And, that is as it should be.

Bush's Anti-Democratic Tactics

An Opinion
Originally published November 16, 2000.

Amid George W. Bush's rhetoric is a stated desire to turn government duties over to private religious charities. This is echoed by conservative columnists across the country.

Besides the sensible argument that charities failed miserably at distributing society's largesse and had to be replaced in many of their activities by the government, there are a fundamental democratic principles at stake in the debate. Charities are profoundly undemocratic institutions. This is especially so for religious charities.

With government, every voter can exercise a say in the functioning of the country, state, or city. By becoming involved, a citizen can make a difference in the policies and practices of our collective undertakings.

The opposite principles are in effect with charities. Charities are often opposed to public involvement. They limit the number that can have a say to protect the functioning of the charity. This is obvious with religious charities which restrict membership to those associated with their fellowship.

The basic act of receiving help from a charity becomes compromised when you are prevented from enacting any change to the charity. You have no standing to seek redress if they make a decision adverse to your interests.

I don't think I would find many Republicans who would disagree with the statement that our society is founded on the three pillars of free markets, democracy, and the rule of law. Yet, these same pillars of our success are at odds with relying on charities to provide services to the poor.

Charities are basically uncompetitive entities. There main concern is often safeguarding the assets they have wrung from their constituency. In this respect, they resemble investment houses more often than active participants in society.

If a charity can find an area where there are no competitors, that is all too often where it will stay. It will avoid the hubbub of the marketplace for the safety of the cloister.

The almseekers are the original conservatives. They will retain what they have and sidestep controversy.

I have already spoken of their undemocratic nature and hinted at their avoidance of the rule of law. Religious charities have used the protection of religion clause of the Constitution to shelter their activities from laws applying regularly to all other segments of our society. This is as the founders intended; no laws abridging the freedom of religion.

Just wait until you are in a position to challenge a charity to provide the services requested by the government and desired by the public. You will have no standing in their hierarchy, no ability to challenge them in court, and no competitors to approach instead.

If George W. Bush succeeds in winning the presidency and lives by his promises, we will experience a profound anti-democratic shift as services are migrated to the charitable sector. What I find amazing is that the implications of this policy are rarely discussed.

America's Conservative Times

An Opinion
Originally published November 17, 2000.

America is in the midst of conservative times. An examination of the election should lead you to the same conclusion.

The biggest issue of this election year was a prescription drug benefit for senior citizens. Regardless of the candidate's sincerity or the merits of their plans, the fact remains that these were conservative, even reactionary, proposals.

One of the lasting successes of our welfare state is that senior citizens are no longer struggling in poverty. Rather, they are one of the most well-off sectors of society. Therefore, prescription drug benefits would increase the wealth of golden geezers.

The Democrats and Republicans were scrambling over each other to increase the wealth of these constituents. This, while poverty among children is an increasingly intractable and devastating problem.

I do not hold either party blameless or in esteem for their stands on this issue. The Democrats are cynically promising to be generous with the ladle while ignoring social problems they have sworn to work on. The Republicans while mouthing the view that government has no role in the problem were as happy with a new social program to call their own.

The only significant difference between the two parties was whether to have the drug benefit be based on the recipient's income. Democrats favor making the benefit universal and, thus, harder to kill. Republicans want it means tested and, theoretically, this will make it more vulnerable to cost cuts in the future. This is really only a difference in degree.

So, as we tell the future of the great presidential race of the year 2000, let us not forget to mention how both parties wrestled each other to be the ones to provide the biggest chunk of federal dollars to a group that is not currently having problems. This is disgraceful.

What is also disgraceful is the amount of corporate welfare riding on this election. Campaign contributions are regarded as investments to soon yield the reward of the capitol capital.

Companies with vital investments in the future of our country should not need the help of our government to survive. Subsidies distort the economic picture of our country. By promoting favoritism within and among industries, and you know that companies donating to campaigns count on the same, the government hurts the economy.

Again, there is not much separating the two parties. The variances are in their friendly industries. Companies pick sides and the parties play the game.

Does it need saying that companies in our booming economy should not require any government assistance? If they do, there is something dreadfully wrong.

Here we are awaiting a president. One who will transfer even more of the nation's wealth to parties not needing help. This meets my definition of reactionary.

The Punditry of Marc Racicot

An Opinion
Originally published November 20, 2000.

Marc Racicot appeared on ABC TV's *This Week* Sunday. He also backed up Bush mouthpiece Karen Hughes in her arguments of vote manipulation. It is increasingly clear that our governor is part of the main Bush team.

I found this performance to be Marc Racicot's lowest level to date. This even eclipses the nadir reached when he was blaming Clinton for causing the year 2000 fires in Montana.

The chief point Mr. Racicot made on *This Week* was that the Bush campaign has fought for the rule of law. In this instance, he argued that the rule of law meant that there should be no hand recounting of ballots.

This view puts Mr. Racicot at odds with Katherine Harris, the Florida secretary of state. On the Florida Department of State web site Ms. Harris states, "...the law provides for automatic recounts, protests, and manual recounts..." Please be satisfied with my statement that Mr. Racicot could find no fault with her partisanship.

This is such a wonderful example of Marc Racicot's tendency to go back to his confrontational legal roots when in a conflict. The issue itself is not the matter. It is whether or not to argue about it. Argument always takes precedence over solution.

Perhaps, it is not enough for Mr. Racicot that Florida, Texas, and Montana law (*Montana Code Annotated*, 13-16-412) all call for the manual recounting of ballots. There is some argument to be made that manual recounting is illegal no matter how far credulity is stretched.

The worst moment of Mr. Racicot's outing on television came as he held up a bag of chads (the little punched out holes made by voting). This amounted to some proof of neglect or treachery in Mr. Racicot's argument. They are punched out holes, for goodness sake. Would saving them really make a difference? It was political theater with our governor performing the show.

Governor Racicot also made the case that counting votes will somehow disadvantage one candidate over the other.

He suggested, as many other Republican flacks and hacks had, that the manual recount would be subjective. This argument dissolves when you consider that if the same standard is applied to all ballots, and it will be without question, then no candidate gains an advantage from true standards of vote tallying.

How am I so certain that standards are being applied and followed? Look to the recounting process. There are Democratic and Republican observers, video cameras, and members of the public raring to report any strange circumstances. I find it funny that with Mr. Racicot's allegations he has not produced any witnesses. This would seem to be desperate lawyering.

Finally, I find the timing of Mr. Racicot's appearance interesting. He takes the stage as the campaign pushes James Baker to the rear. James Baker exits as his argument of "let's get on with making Bush president" recedes. This damaged Mr. Baker's credibility so that he needs some time out of the spotlight to regain his stature.

Racicot brings his new arguments of the unfair recount and their obedience to the law along with his bag of chads, which would be beneath the dignity of a former Secretary of State. Racicot also has the status of being a Bush peer and not a crony of his father. This can counter the criticism that George W. Bush seeks the security of this father's old hands in crisis. Marc Racicot represents a new generation of leadership.

It is somewhat thrilling to see Montana's Governor on the national scene. When his role is so melodramatic and hackneyed, it gives shame to every citizen of Montana.

Supreme Wrangling

An Opinion
Originally published November 21, 2000.

      In contrast to Marc Racicot's ill-reasoned parade of chads, the Florida Supreme Court provided temperance and forbearance to an otherwise contentious and fractious battle for the ballot of Florida. Listening to the proceedings today broadcast by KUFM and NPR I was grateful to hear the issues being questioned on their merits.

      For those of you not fortunate enough to have caught the Supreme Court session, let me encapsulate their lines of questioning. I know most of the justices were appointed by Democrats but I think they were after points of law to guide an impartial decision.

      Chief Justice Charles T. Wells set the tone for the discussion when he stated that,

"...the real parties of interest are the voters..." His main line of questioning, indeed, the main line of questioning of all the justices, was whether there was a specific date to uphold in sanctioning the balloting.

There seemed to be general agreement that a date of December 12th was the outside date in order to certify the electors for the state of Florida. This would still allow for contests before the electoral college voting date of December 18th.

However, taking this date as an outside mark there was little to guide the justices about a more current mark. Taking the date seven days from the election as a guide there seemed to be confusion about the inclusion of recounted votes. At one point justice Major B. Harding asked for "any record" of interest to their guidance. As an alternative he suggested "divine intervention".

This is a good example of their second most popular line of questioning. They strove to find out how all of this would work. Would a recount not count if it was after the seven day deadline? Uppermost in their minds seemed to be the issues of fairness to the voters. They didn't want Florida's electors to go uncertified and lack representation in the electoral college.

The third line of questioning sought the boundaries of discretion to ignore certain voters and its associated reasoning of whether the Secretary of State used her discretion wisely.

The final queries related to mistakes in the balloting. This surprised me because I had not expected this to be an issue before the court. Justice Major B. Harding stated that it was well-known that, "...voters do not follow instructions...". He followed this up with examples of past court decisions finding that where voting intention is seen, it counts.

The case overall amounted to a balancing of recounts versus deadlines with little to base a decision upon. Now, who did well and who did not.

As a team, the Democratic and Gore lawyers appeared to have it together more than the Republican-Bush squad. The Bush lawyers sounded more shrill and less relaxed. The Gore bunch, in maintaining their stance of allowing recounts statewide, accounted for the majority of the fairness arguments. Whether they had a leg to stand on remains to be seen.

This judge gives the decision on points to Gore. Here is how I see it playing out. The justices will not stop the hand recounts. The justices will allow dimpled ballots. Once this decision is made, hand recounts will sweep the state.

Strike it up

A Potpourri
Originally published November 22, 2000.

Workers of the *Seattle Times* and the *Seattle Post-Intelligencer* went on strike yesterday. About two minutes past their strike time a new paper emerged called the *Union Record*.

Even though the spirits of the strikers are high, history tells us that this could be the beginning of the end for one of the papers. While the pressure to achieve higher pay in the Seattle area drove on the strikers, the example of being able to produce an Internet paper quickly and easily displays the vulnerability of old media giants.

Their victory could prove Pyrrhic if they kill off a paper, as has happened in many cities, or if they turn enough people to alternative media that they bite off a substantial enough chunk of revenue to prevent an increase of salary. Neither of these outcomes is pleasing to either party I am sure. Here's to hoping they solve their problems quickly.

I saw an incredible dance performance by the Lily Cai Chinese Dance Company as part of the 17th Annual Mansfield Conference at the University of Montana. A benefit showing for various Missoula hunger charities, the performance was breathtaking and spellbinding.

Lily Cai said that when she came to America people encouraged her to quit dance. She realized her great talents for choreography and costume design and we were able to enjoy her muse due to her stubbornness.

The troupe danced both historically based dances and contemporary pieces. They used long flowing scarves to create walls of fire and what appeared to be chinese characters. Along with raising money for charity the tickets to the event were free to children and this was an incredible gift to the community.

Heard on the radio Tuesday afternoon was a small story about the Bush campaign seeking a judge's ruling to have the court seize the chads from ballot counting rooms. This would have entail impounding vacuum bags and trash cans.

I can think of no other reason for this effort than to provide a little cover for Marc Racicot's idiocy. Is it any wonder that this case was disposed quickly without the judge ordering seizure of dustbins?

It seems queer that even though Bush is ahead in the vote count and shows no signs of falling behind his legal team is grasping at straws. It could just be a factor of trying to show that they are earning all of the money being thrown their way.

Meanwhile, as we are going to upload, I have heard that the Supreme Court is allowing an extension in the deadline to Sunday or Monday. They did not rule about how the recounts were being conducted.

It looks to this observer like we may be nearing an end to the 2000 presidential odyssey. His initials just might be G.W.B.

Happy Thanksgiving

A Revelation
Originally published November 23, 2000.

  If one holiday symbolizes America it is Thanksgiving. A holiday that can be enjoyed by a person of any religious background. A holiday that does not require any kind of patriotic display. Thanksgiving manages to be both spiritual and deeply praising of our country.

  Thanksgiving is not a holiday we share with another country.* It is uniquely American. Perhaps, it is a holiday associated with Americans overseas.

  Think about the wartime films of Americans enjoying their turkey as they

---

* Canadians have their own Thanksgiving, too. 2012 note.

stamp out the Nazis, fight communists, or put down dictators. I know my mind always wanders to the people in uniform and in service for our country. Here's hoping they have a great day.

Being in a mood of reminiscence brought on by the holiday season I would like to share three special Thanksgivings. They weren't the greatest necessarily but each was memorable.

While an exchange student in New Zealand my host parents hosted a Thanksgiving dinner for me to make me feel at home. This was a touching gesture and reminds me of their love. I hope they are well and healthy.

The next Thanksgiving took place during the first Movie Marathon. The Movie Marathon involved watching 72 hours of movies straight through. During the first day of the Marathon some of the folks stopped the movies and went to partake in a potluck. For some reason I didn't feel like eating at all that day. I don't think it had so much to do with appetite as with a little self-sacrifice being good for the soul.

The final Thanksgiving involved three single friends and me. We were sitting around my house on Thanksgiving day. None of us had any money and as we realized that we all might miss out on any good eating someone came up with the idea to go to the Thanksgiving meal provided as charity. We went and had a wonderful time.

Our gathering of friends became a meal with universal brotherhood as we ate, laughed, and listened to incredible clarinet music provided by a band playing through one of those old star-within-a-circle radio microphones. They had enough food left to provide us each with a another meal to take home for later.

In the years since I have helped deliver meals to shut-ins and driven homeless to Christmas meals to atone for my use of charity. In some ways it is always as much fun to give as to receive and I hope I have made some people's days.

Gather your family together and enjoy a fabulous repast. Happy Thanksgiving, from *The Outrider.*

Happy Shopping

An Exposition
Originally published November 24, 2000.

The day after Thanksgiving is the biggest shopping day of the year in the United States. Those of us bombarded with advertisements for the past few days realize this fact too well. It is the offical opening of the consumption season.

For the next five weeks or so we will undergo our festival of buying and selling as never before. Each year seems to grow slightly more absurd in its dimensions.

Whether or not there is a ticklish Elmo or a baby in a cabbage patch waiting to become the next hot toy, this season promises to be the largest ever in terms of total spending. Already, there have been musings in the media that this holiday will not measure up to last year's phenomenal growth. This year we will have to be satisfied with an average increase.

There is something disturbing to me about all of this spending and giving. Perhaps, it is the result of anti-materialistic fables of my upbringing like the Grinch. Speaking of which, how hypocritical is it to plaster the Grinch's likeness over every holiday good available?

I suppose crazy commercialization is the fate of all emotive symbols of holiday love such as Scrooge and the Grinch. It is the way of our society to use anything, no matter whether it is opposed, to continue its growth.

But when it comes right down to it, is all of this purchasing so terrible. Sure, you will probably end up with an ugly sweater or two. But isn't your loss, some charity's gain in a newer good.

Edward Bellamy in his utopian book *Looking Backward: From 2000 to 1887* posits that "buying and selling" are "an education in self-seeking at the expense of others." A similar view was propounded by Karl Marx. Their fear of the market led to solutions being imposed in certain countries which invariably made things much worse.

Contrast this with the cheerful optimism of Adam Smith who conjectures:

It is not from the benevolence of the

butcher, the brewer, or the baker, that we expect our dinner, but from their regard to their own interest. We address ourselves, not to their humanity but to their self-love and never talk to them of our own necessities but of their advantages.

In his scheme we are glad to make purchases because this creates and stabilizes the market. Luckily, we have stayed true to his view and avoided disastrous utopian trials.

Even though we can rely on the market to provide for ourselves and our kin, isn't the market a frightening, boisterous place especially at this time? Indeed, I find it so on occasion.

This is also the market telling us to go home and live some activities with our loved ones. The best experiences are unavailable for purchase.

Return to Denver, Part One

An Experience
Originally published November 27, 2000.

       As I prepare to return to Denver I thought I would relate my reminiscence of the last time I visited the Mile High City. Whenever I have been to Denver I have had bad experiences. The last, however, proved to be extremely unfortunate for the city.

       It was April of 1999, more than a year-and-a-half from today. I was in town for a telecommunications conference. In the shadow of the US West (remember them?) building I attended classes on publicizing telephone and internet services while I studied for my MBA in the evenings.

       The anniversary of the Oklahoma bombing was April 19th. Cities across the nation had been preparing for some type of terrorist attack to occur on that day. Denver was no exception and the papers carried articles about readiness for the worst.

The night of the 19th I observed some of these precautions firsthand. The hotel I was in was across the street from a federal building. It looked like they emptied out the fleet to park cars one deep all the way across the building. This was a precaution against an Oklahoma type bombing.

Overhead, a white helicopter circled languidly. This lasted until about midnight and, I suppose, the presumption that the worst threat was over.

As a new day dawned I was sprung from the conference and had some time to experience Denver before my flight home. I decided to walk down to the U.S. Mint building, now, apparently not a target.

I tried to go in the exit door of the Mint and was told to walk around. I joined a tour of the Mint and was led through by a more than usually nervous guard. I think, in retrospect, they already knew of the attack at Columbine High School. They were nervous because no one knew of the scale of the threat.

Was the report from the high school the first feint in a larger plan? I will write more about the assault and the aftermath tomorrow.

In other news, I saw Marc Racicot on NBC's *Meet the Press*. He set some new records for political hypocrisy. In contrast to last week's appearance on ABC's *This Week*. he was now accepting of the manual recount. In a wonderful example of someone's own rhetoric tripping themselves he proffered this syllogism.

> "Florida law provides for a manual recount. You must count all of the ballots."

And,

> "Anything allowed for by law we have fully supported."

He *is* a lawyer after all.

Return to Denver, Part Two

An Experience
Originally published November 28, 2000.

When last we left the tale Denver was in the midst of a tragedy. I had no idea it was occurring. The officers of the Mint seemed to be all too aware.

As I left the Mint, I began the journey back to my hotel. Along the way to and from the Mint were gigantic billboards of Charlton Heston. He was representing the National Rifle Association which was to be meeting in Denver the next week.

The first I became aware of the unfolding situation was people watching television through shop windows from the sidewalk. I stopped and asked a man what was happening and he said there had been a shooting.

I noticed people speaking on the streets. Earlier it had been a warm spring day and the mood was gentle and enjoyable. Word of the shooting changed the tone of the day.

I stopped into a shop to purchase some Stephanie's Chocolates. They knew it was at a school and were worried about their children. We made some small talk and I continued on my way.

I went to The Palm restaurant on the ground floor for the hotel. Sounds of the television displaying footage of Columbine High School filled the bar. Conversations ranged with speculation. Who was behind this and what were their motives?

On a personal level the news of the assault scared me and I retreated into myself as I ate my simple meal. I did not want to hear about the massacre. I downed a couple of glasses of iced tea and then went up to the desk to retrieve my bags.

My nervousness continued as I rode to the airport in the Super Shuttle. By this time the attack was reckoned by the riders to be contained to the high school. The talk was of the shame of it all.

However, on the way to the airport I saw more police officers than I had ever seen in my life. The driver of the shuttle commented on their proliferation. I assume they were carrying out a master plan that had been devised in preparation for a terrorist plot on April 19.

One positive of all of the planning for terrorism was that Denver was probably extremely ready for the tragedy that occurred on April 20. More tomorrow about Denver and Littleton.

Return to Denver, Pt. Three

An Experience
Originally published November 29, 2000.

I was on my way to the airport. The Littleton massacre had already come and gone. Tactical teams were in Columbine High School and clearing room after arduous room.

Children were at the hospital. The scale of the tragedy became clear as the police risked themselves to move through the school.

Pulling up to Denver International Airport the shuttle driver said in a discussion of the architecture of the building that it looked like it was "tepees put up by drunken Indians." The great hall of the DIA, I found frightening and inhumanly large and foreboding. Perhaps it was the slaughter occurring across town. I did not like the building.

Maybe it was the iced tea. I carried my fright to the airplane and flew out scared.

Flying down to Denver on Monday I had to face my fear. Thinking of it during my more lucid moments I think I had come to associate the horror of the Columbine shootings and bombings with airline travel.

It is one of the powerful axioms of human nature that by confronting our fears we conquer them. By flying to Denver on Monday I got to look the death of the students in the face. I had to resolve my wariness of both Denver and flying. By writing this series I had to examine my thoughts for threads of compassion and forgiveness.

Let's look the killing full in the face. More than 30 people were wounded. 12 people were killed.

A bomb was detonated in the parking lot. A bomb had gone off in the library. The total number of bombs found at the school and the killer's homes was 51.

Eric Harris and Dylan Klebold, two teenage boys, plotted and enacted a major act of violence on their classmates. They showed no sympathy for their victims. Rather, they targeted athletes and reserved their cruelty for students who begged for mercy.

In all likelihood they planned the

attack to take place on Hitler's birthday. They left behind carnage.

Return to Denver, Part Four

An Experience
Originally published November 30, 2000.

The news was reporting yesterday that there is a settlement offer in the works for the victims of the Columbine massacre. The figure given was $1.6 million to be split between 37 families.

Doing the math, that amount figures to less than $50,000 per family. The money is coming from homeowner's policies of the Harris and Klebold families.

I am sure that some families will get more than other. Of course, the money will never put the terrors back that were unleashed. It is sadly inadequate.

Perhaps, it is the American way to put a price tag on every event. A tragedy of this magnitude comes down to $1.6 mill.

The lawyers always look for the deep pocket in every situation. I had no idea my renter's policy might cover my daughter going ballistic. It is probably worth the money to the insurance company just for the riddance of the nuisance of the carrion followers.

Driving by Wheat Ridge High School this morning my friend said of Wheat Ridge, "It's nice. It ain't Littleton." Was he right? Another friend has a sticker that says, "We are all Columbine."

I think the fright is that this is liable to occur anywhere, anytime. I believe this to be real. It is something the NRA wishes would go away, but violence will be done.

We are an extremely violent society. Violence is sanctioned from the White House to the poorhouse. We must live with our acts and violence will be done.

In an unrelated story breaking the same time as the settlement talks the news reported the finding of six bomblets of nerve gas at the chemical weapon area here in Colorado. These bombs are illegal according to the rules of war. Yet, we produced them in association with our role in NATO.

Our fervent desire for safety has yielded a dreadful toll of horrific devices to maim and destroy. When children learn from our example, should we really be surprised?

Return to Denver, Part Five

An Experience
Originally published December 1, 2000.

Knock on wood. I have had a good experience during my time in Denver.

I don't know what I expected. I thought maybe I had a Denver jinx. I also suspected fate would find me here again to face my fears. I couldn't go on fearing air travel and hating Denver.

This has been such a personal journey, I hope you forgive me dear reader. I know writing this series has helped me to exorcise some demons. I beg your indulgence for personal salvation.

On a civic level can there also be redemption? I think there can. Here is why.
We live in a country today that has had

to come to an agreement with our greatest enemy. The cold war has been ten years dead. Along with our peace, we have cut the number of our nuclear weapons.

The six bomblets in Colorado were only revealed because we are in a safer time now than we have ever been. Their eventual destruction will be due to our human capacity to forgive.

There is something else the destruction will illustrate. It will show that peaceful solutions make everyone safer. We do not become safer by refusing to face our fears. We become safer by realizing our vulnerability and joining with others to solve our problems.

I wrote yesterday about America's violent culture. This is true. It is also possible that America will continue along the path to peace and can become a non-violent society.

The end of the cold war shows that America does have the power to forgive. America does not need so many redundant bombs or nerve gas bomblets.

Looking toward our future. America is not doomed to violence. We can take heart from our constitution that in reference to Armies the document said that Congress has the power to raise the same. With respect to a Navy, Congress may provide for one. Neither are considered necessities.

America's charter was built wisely

enough to provide for lasting peace. Here's hoping we find a way to bring it about.

December in Montana

An Experience
Originally published December 4, 2000.

The cold is forcefully with us now. We shiver as we walk outside and go to work. The trees barrenly expand with frost. Birds scatter from bush to bush for the remaining berries of summer.

Ice builds up on the steps to my apartment. The sun does not have enough strength to melt the previous days' snow. Also, the sun's angle is too precarious to facilitate much in the way of direct shine to the steps.

Starting the car in morning has become a chore with ice and frost needing to be scraped. Whether it is true frost or those ice storms or Italian ice; the frozen moisture might take a good five minutes to release off a vehicle my size.

In addition, If we have had an ice storm both of my front doors seize up in the lock mechanism. This means I will either have to enter from a rear door and then push out on a front door after I have climbed over the seat or drive to work without opening a front door. The advantage of the second method is that, at least, I don't have to wait for the ice within the door to melt from the puny efforts of my car heater.

Chances are, we will see some severely subzero temperatures for a week or two. Will they come tomorrow? or February? One never knows. When they rush in we should be able to track them coming over the border from Canada and the high arctic.

The geese are no longer seen flying south. Apparently, some have decided to hole up in Wheat Ridge, Colorado for the winter as I saw quite a few down there.

Ski resorts are still waiting for enough snow to open. Ski swaps and sales are in full swing as people get geared up to schuss.

Who could neglect to mention the bombardment by fund-raisers? This part of the year is serious business for those raising money and no one will be left unasked.

As I was shopping at Osco on Saturday the Salvation Army kettle had a lovely serenade by an excellent singer. It made me drop some money in the pot.

Here's hoping you have been invited to a party or two. The holiday cheerfulness should be welcomed in all of our homes.

As we celebrate, let us remember our loved ones and demonstrate our love.

Blacklist...What Blacklist?

An Bill Review
Originally published December 5, 2000.

Let us look to the bills being introduced for the 2001 session of the Montana legislature. First up is Senate Bill 1 introduced by Duane Grimes, Republican of Clancy.

My guess is that this bill comes straight from the Chamber of Commerce brain trust. It represents an attempt to shield businesses from lawsuits alleging blacklisting.

The bill starts innocently enough with language requiring an employer to provide a written explanation of their employee's dismissal. This modifies previous language that allowed an employer an option of whether to respond to an employee's request for an explanation.

The former language was interesting in that if the employer did not respond to an employee's request for the reason for their dismissal, then the employer had to hold his peace. This was wishy-washy enough to allow the employer to change their mind at any time, but it had an intriguing logic. If the employer had nothing to say about a dismissal, they should keep their mouth shut.

The prospects of compelling an employer to produce a reason for dismissal are even more delightful. I wonder why no one thought of this sooner. Shouldn't every employer be compelled to provide a reason for dismissal? It would simplify unemployment issues. There would be no guesswork.

One part that gives me pause is the requirement to let the former employer know that this statement can be used in potential litigation. Shouldn't that be a given?

Again, this employer response can be modified at any time. Sure, this protects employers when, say, an old employee's misdeeds continue to come to life. But, can't this be tied to a requirement to notify the employee of the change?

Where the bill gets a little *1984* for me is the language that a blacklist depends on its being an actual list, whether written or oral. Can one person be a list? Is this just a convenient backdoor for employers to avoid a blacklisting charge? Only your local

Chamber knows for sure.

Specifically in the bill is language that "individual employment references do not constitute blacklisting." This is in opposition to the current logical language of the statute. I am afraid Mr. Grimes is trying to pull a fast one folks.

This bill completely unfetters an employer to change his reason for dismissal without any notice and to bad talk you to potential employers. Any recriminations disappear.

Congratulations, Mr. Grimes! You have taken the lead for most asinine bill thus reviewed.

Do You Want Fries With That?

A Bill Review
Originally published December 6, 2000.

We continue looking at the bills being introduced for the 2001 session of the Montana legislature. Next up is Senate Bill 18 introduced by Jerry O'Neil of Kalispell.

An intriguing bill in that it could cut both ways. Is this really a destruction of rights? Or, is this a fulfillment of those rights?

The bill basically provides that a criminal background check is performed when a person renews a driver's license. This serves the purpose of allowing a person to get a gun endorsement on their license. Possessed of this endorsement, the licensee can now purchase a firearm with no further check required.

Originally, this struck me as an invasion of privacy. Do we really want the government getting a blank check to delve into a citizen's criminal history? After all, what does driving a car have to do with shooting a gun?

However, as I thought about it further, I could see some logic to it. Why not one simple background check? Then, you can buy guns to your heart's delight. Tie it in with hunting licenses. You can't hunt, if you don't have a gun.

One poor part of the bill is that this background check would only last for five years rather than the eight years for driver's license. Why not match them up somehow? A five-year driver's license and background check are a match made in heaven.

On further reflection, I smell the long arm of the law, the iron fist in the velvet glove. Let us not make government too efficient. By having things wonderfully muddled, we retain what little freedom we have left.

Sock It To Me?

An Opinion
Originally published December 7, 2000.

We take a break from bill reviews to delve into the heart of insurance company darkness.

With George W. Bush's supposed election the pipers will need to be paid. He cost good money and now comes the return.

Last week I received notice that Blue Cross Blue Shield of Montana proposed to raise my group insurance rates by over one-third. That is no misprint. They asked for a raise of over 35%.

I guess I could have two thoughts about this matter. The first is that BCBS is so completely incompetent that they miscalculated extremely poorly for the last several years. The second is that they take the putative Bush election as an opportunity to gouge the living daylights out of their customers. Both could be true.

Nationwide, I have read that insurance rates are expected to see double-digit inflation. This is no coincidence. Gore's disguised breathings of universal health care made the medical establishment cluster heavily behind Bush. With a possible four years of no medical reform the best profits await.

The theory of the insurance companies is probably one of wanting to get their best shot in while they have a chance. Somewhat tamed during the Clinton administration they smell the blood of their insured and are moving in for the kill. By raising rates drastically now they can maybe get another one or two outrageous increases before they have to settle down for a Bush re-election.

This is the harbinger of the reign of greed to be unleashed by Bush's election.

Whence Cheney?

An Opinion
Originally published December 8, 2000.

We maintain our break from bill reviews to excavate a mystery. Is Dick Cheney a Wyoming resident?

Shortly before Dick Cheney accepted the vice presidential nomination from George W. Bush he flew to Wyoming to register to vote. As far as I can tell, this was his sole act to establish residency.

I heard on the radio that a group was trying to challenge his Wyoming residency in Dallas court. There are several potential problems with the Dick Cheney residency question. The first and greatest is that the members of the electoral college from a certain state, say Texas, are forbidden from voting for a presidential and vice presidential candidate from the same state.

If Cheney wasn't actually a resident of Wyoming, then he and George Bush would have to forfeit their electoral votes from Texas. This could, in theory, throw the election to Gore.

Let's cut through all the crap. Dick Cheney lives with his wife in Virginia. He has for years. He probably goes to Texas often enough to maintain residency there to avoid state income taxes. That was, at least, until this year. Then he became a Wyoming resident by visiting the state for a day.

The two reasons he became a Wyoming resident again were to avoid the electoral college problem and the perception of a presidential ticket consisting of two Texas oilmen.

At the time, I reviewed Wyoming laws and found that they provided for potential perjury charges for making a false statement of residency. I thought I might write this up but frankly I guess my opinion is that our age is so jaded no one even cares if Mr. Cheney tells the truth or not.

Basically, in the constitution-loving heart of my innocent soul I find Mr. Cheney guilty of grand cynicism and included lesser charges. He lives in Virginia but claims residency for purposes of greed. When it served his purposes to defeat the constitution he showed no compunction in signing what could and should be considered a false document.

Going Mental

A Bill Review
Originally published December 11, 2000.

We return to bill reviews to check out Senate Joint Resolution 2 proposed by Mignon Waterman, Democrat of Helena.

Joint Resolutions are the Prozac of the legislature. They make everybody feel good. But, do they really accomplish anything?

Successful resolutions are usually concerning issues that most people agree need a solution. However, no one can agree on a solution. So, along comes a resolution with a proposed answer but no funding. Every legislator can get a warm fuzzy for passing such a device along with a good night's sleep knowing that the status quo remains.

Senate Joint Resolution 2 seems cut from this positive cloth. It concerns the needs of the mentally ill within our criminal justice system. There should be widespread agreement that a good proportion of our prison population is both mentally ill and ill-treated.

A word about the form of resolutions. They usually precede with a number of "whereas" statements that can generally be taken as facts. This is the statement of the problem. This resolution probably does not lay on enough facts. Perhaps that is a strategy to allow further embellishment as it gets crafted later.

The next portion of a resolution will contain the proposed solution to the difficulty. This can be as simple as asking the U.S. Congress to take some action. Lots of lawmakers can agree that it would be fine if someone else took some action about this dreadful conundrum.

In the case of SJ 2 the "resolved" portion takes the point of view of a parent sending all of the kids back out to the sandbox to place nice with each other. Certainly it would be great if a greater awareness of, sensitivity to, and treatment for mental illness existed at all levels of our criminal justice system.

Ultimately, resolutions do not work because they fail to carry the power of money with them. Without a checkbook behind it, any idea is just so much thought.

Here's Your Horoscope

Best of the Web
Originally published December 12, 2000.

       The best place to get you horoscope is put together by Astrodienst AG, a German company, at www.astro.com. Although there are many reports available for purchase the site offers a decent selection of free charts and reports including a very detailed daily horoscope.

       The level of detail for a daily horoscope I have not seen beaten by another site on the Internet. Include the fact that it is personalized based upon birth data you supply and you have an excellent place for astrological information that should please someone with extensive knowledge of the zodiac and its mysteries.

       For those of you who enjoy the simple

pleasure of a few clipped paragraphs in the news, this is probably much too intensive for your needs. It takes a minute or two to give your birth data and the place of your birth. After you have set up a profile a number of free horoscopes are available.

Do you want to have a perspective on your future? Astro offers a forecast which looks several years ahead to a number of star aspects in your life.

How about the chances for you and your lover? Partner reports, as well as their AstroClick composite chart, are available.

The AstroClick charts on love and partnership are fascinating. By allowing the viewer to select various aspects or house positions by a simple click a person can gain a greater knowledge of astrology simply by viewing elements of their own chart.

One of the more esoteric attraction is the ability to find what are termed your VIP Astro-Twins. These are people who possess roughly the same birth positions, specifically the ascendant and sun. I looked at mine and did not know any of the VIP's but was fascinated to find out more about them.

If you find yourself with some extra time in the morning or evening a trip to www.astro.com is well worth it.

Satan's Little Helper

A Diversion
Originally published December 13, 2000.

Today, I wanted to look up the word "satan" at www.m-w.com. In my mind it always seems to have an extra "n" before the "t". I remember the first time I saw it I pronounced it as "satin". It sure looks more like satin. Instead, it sounds to me like "Saint N." Which I think is ironic. The idea that the prince of darkness' name begins with the sound of the word saint.

Anyway, after finding that Merriam-Webster's does not consider satan to have an n sound before the t, I noticed some of the side bars. Those are the little links that most web sites are afflicted with these days. The interesting part is that many of these places do not anticipate a search for "satan" or the like and you get strange results.

A good example was the side bar that said, 'Get to know "satan" at brittanica.com.' I've always wanted to get closer with him. Can they show me how?

Having gone to brittanica.com I noticed that they offered further ways to relate to the dark one. 'Want great prices on satan at top rated stores? Visit BizRate!' Apparently, businessmen get to visit that special room in the back.

How about, 'Visit the Brittanica Shopping Channel to shop across the web for satan.' What do you think he might like for Christmas?

Looking at Yahoo! I found this palindrome, 'Satan Oscillate my Metallic Sonatas.' Barnes & Noble will search for "satan". When I took them up on this I located 317 titles. *My Date with Satan* by Stacey Richter came up first. Ginia Bellafante of *Time* says she "brings a wacky imagination." Satan would be pleased.

Trying Lycos I got the scary response that 'People who did this search also searched for: Horn Body Parts.' Also, they offered shopping for over 60 products about "satan".

Finally, Altavista presented a cornucopia of satanic references. These included: 'Shop the web for "satan".' 'Find "satan" and millions of other cool items at eBay!' If these weren't enough you can 'set

you own price for "satan" at uBid.com.'

Pulping Up the Volume

A Review
Originally published December 14, 2000.

I picked up a free copy of *OUTDOORPULP* at REI today. This is the second issue of this new tabloid. It seems they are shooting for a biweekly publication schedule.

I must say the issue is attractively laid out. The front page has a gripping 3/4-page ice-climbing photograph. Inside, the middle spread features two more full-page photos. The snowboarding shot is particularly spectacular.

The story selection ranged from event coverage to a profile of Montanan Levi Leipheimer who is a member of the US Postal Service Tour de France team. The feature story concerned an ice-climbing competition in Hyalite Canyon near Bozeman.

The editor John Ross focuses on breezy light articles in keeping with a general tone of fun and excitement about the outdoors. Some interesting filler articles about national and worldwide outdoor adventurers flesh out the article content.

An outdoor event calendar should prove useful for finding your pleasure. Combine with some event outcome reporting and you could while away a few moments with this newspaper.

Their business strategy includes selling subscriptions and/or memberships, as well as providing free circulation. They are even offering an expensive mountain bike as a prospective sweepstakes prize to a lucky subscriber.

OUTDOORPULP represents a great resource for the outdoor minded. I probably won't pick one up regularly. It is a little too organized for my outdoor taste. I prefer small group or solitary activities. However, if I had some friends coming in from out of town I would want to get one to find out about special events.

Bush and Montana

An Opinion
Originally published December 15, 2000.

Now that George W. Bush has sewn up the presidency what may we in Montana expect his impact to be? While there may be a few differences I think the status quo will roughly hold.

As much as Republicans will want to open the West, there is not too much left to exploit. Trees that aren't there can't be cut.

The salmon-killing dams would probably have stayed whether Gore or Bush became president. Renters of public lands will not be required to pay anywhere near market value.

Military bases will not make a miraculous comeback. Microsoft will be broken apart. Boeing will merge with another defense contractor.

Gun control will remain much the same, ineffective and inefficient. Prisons will continue to expand. Schools will continue to economize.

The lack of welfare as we knew it will go on showing cracks and spinning more children into poverty. The need for food banks will increase. Job training and assistance will go begging.

All of these items were to remain the same whether Gore or Bush won. Bush's presidency will not make much difference in these issues.

Patronage Primer

A Theory
Originally published December 18, 2000.

Let's take a look at the art of political patronage in the naughties. Where the loyal and acceptable are awarded in the open and the loyal and tarnished are thrown a bone out back.

With the loss in Washington state of Senator Slade Gorton, words are flying that he may be picked to be Secretary of the Interior for George W. Bush. Popular wisdom has it that our own Marc Racicot could be tapped to be Attorney General.

This makes me wonder what Conrad Burns may have been rewarded with if he had been defeated. I think his racist remarks would have kept him from any sort of public or semi-public position. He may have rated a sinecure of the kind bestowed on Lieutenant Governor Kolstad after his unsuccessful run at Max Baucus. Kolstad became head of the International Boundary Commission; which is a fancy way of saying that he was in charge of cutting the grass along the Canadian and American border.

Let's look at Marc Racicot. He was whispered to be a leading contender for the Interior post before Gorton's defeat. The Interior Secretary is usually a prominent westerner like Bruce Babbitt.

But Racicot would have some serious problems being confirmed as Interior Secretary. There are the thousand dead buffaloes from Yellowstone and ample footage to convince a wind sock public that Racicot was a bigger butcher than Colonel Sanders.

With a post like Attorney General the dead animal images would not be such an effective borker. However, there may yet be a twist to Mr. Racicot goes to Washington.

Racicot was front and center in the propaganda campaign to win George W. Bush the White House. Like a good foot soldier he hoisted his bag of chads and trudged the many miles of talk show corridors to carry a message to millions.

Now, it is payback time. Racicot expects his position. Will he get it or will he get a surprise?

The Democrats may demand a scapegoat. Sure, they have accepted their loss but not without suspecting some trickery by the Bush brothers in the Florida vote.

The Democrats' wrath will need to satiated. Giving Racicot a great old-fashioned borking should just about do the trick. Who better than the front man with the chads?

If that happens, as it might, Racicot can look forward to a back-office position at the Republican National Committee rebending paper clips.

The Senseless

Best of the Web
Originally published December 19, 2000.

The U.S. Census Bureau is wonderful enough to provide the public with information about ourselves. Who are we Montanans?

The Census has a new service on their web site called QuickFacts. Okay, so they aren't English majors. At least, they are providing the data in easily digestible nuggets.

Stopping by to examine the Montana information in the QuickFacts section I learned some fascinating facts quickly. For instance, while popular wisdom has it that Montana has a high proportion of college graduates the figures tell a different story. Our percentage of college graduates is

19.8% well below the national 20.3%.

Not only are we dumber than average but we are deluded enough to think we are actually smarter. All the news isn't bad. We better the national percentage of high school graduates 81% to 75.2%.

Our population grew faster than the nation's in the 90's. Montana gained 10.5% with the country waddling along at 9.6%.

The next few numbers tell a story most Montanans are familiar with. Our median household income is $6,000 below the national. Our percent in poverty is greater at 15.8% to 13.8%. For children the tale is the same with 22% of them in poverty compared to 20.8% in the United States.

One item I find fascinating is that our retail sales per capita are only slightly below the nation's at $8,853 to $9,190. What this means is that we are really trying our best to keep up with the country in our consumption habits.

Our income may be at 82% of the national but our retail spending is up there at 96%. We will sacrifice to shop.

Spaced Out

Best of the Web
Originally published December 20, 2000.

One of my favorite daily stops on the web is the Nasa web site. I am a particular fan of the Astronomy Picture of the Day.

Today's picture is a time-lapse movie of stars at the center of the universe and how they are swiftly moving. All of this adds up to the theory that there is a black hole at the center of our galaxy.

The Pictures of the Day often find their way onto my computer wallpaper. I especially liked yesterday's. The aurorae of Jupiter are spectacular. What's up with those magnetic flux tubes? I would have appreciated more of an explanation of those.

The NASA site almost seems like a

universe unto itself. I feel like I have just begun to scratch the surface. There is ample room to spend a few hours roaming without repetition.

One of my recent fascinations is the International Space Station. Did you know it is called that because the nations could not agree on a name?

The NASA headquarters for the space station yielded the tidbit that the current crew has been in space for 50 days. That's a long while without a decent shower.

For a moment there my fascination with the ISS led me to consider constructing a model of it. I found The Space Store to contain an astounding range of models of the ISS. Some may be constructed or you can have them build it for you.

Give your mind a break from the earthbound. If you'll pardon me, my flux tube awaits.

Bork Silent, Bork Deep

A Speculation
Originally published December 21, 2000.

I have just received news that Marc Racicot turned down the position of Attorney General for George W. Bush. Why would he do something like that if he had worked his whole life to get to this position?

I would recommend infrequent readers take a moment to peruse our Patronage Primer before continuing with this article. Okay, did you read it. Good. Now, let's proceed.

I would posit that Marc Racicot was given the silent bork down in Austin. Here is how I imagine it went down.

George welcomes Marc in to the "Rind" office. "Thank you, for being my stalwart foot soldier during this campaign."

"You're welcome, George. You know that as faithfully as I have served you, I have never once mentioned wanting a position in the new Bush administration."

"That is true, Marc. Not even a wudge or a nink has left my browage in your direction hinting vaguely at patronage that could be yours for your service."

"You're the greatest, George. I would gladly walk on coals to tie your shoes. Please don't construe that to mean you would ever have to repay my kindness."

"Disfortunately Marc, when I met with Gore he said I would have to let you slide or he would bork you."

"You're not serious."

"I'm afraid I am. We are just going to say I offered you the AG slot and you turned it down for personal reasons."

"Oh, George. It was the chads, wasn't it?"

"Oh, Marc. He knew you were my favorite."

Christmas Spectacular

A Review
Originally published December 22, 2000.

On Wednesday, December 20, 2000 I attended the Paxson first, second, and third grades and the deaf education class presenting a program of Christmas music. I'm pleased to say I greatly appreciated the program.

First up was the Deaf Education Class. They presented a play about Santa being late for Christmas. They followed this with a song called *Hurry Santa!*.

The kids did a wonderful job. There was some stumbling with lines. Over all, they gave an excellent performance.

Let me take this opportunity to congratulate the school and our society for allowing deaf children to participate more fully in activities. Bringing all members of the public together from an early age has been a welcome change from the time of my youth.

My daughter has been learning sign language since kindergarten. I hope this helps her to make a friend that she would not have otherwise. A benefit for both children I would think.

When the children were finished singing their song the audience made the sign language gesture for applause. Could this be anything but the children having taught their parents something?

Next up were the first graders. Their first song was a Hanukkah song. This, too, is a change from my era.

Celebration of the Jewish tradition should be honored. Inclusion of the community will make us stronger.

My congratulations to Ms. Callan. She is the hardworking and effacing music teacher to the students of Paxson elementary along with several other schools.

A great time was had by all the parents. We were able to see the things that are right with our community.

Merry Christmas

An Appreciation
Originally published December 25, 2000.

Before I jump in to the general discussion of Christmas I'd like to take a moment for an aside about another Paxson school event. I attended an all class sing-along on Friday.

On my drive over to the school I was feeling depressed. Holidays can do that to a person. Certainly, I am not immune from the influence of the enforced jollity. It creates a countervailing need to rebel.

Top that off with being late to the event. My computer alarm had gone off but I had somehow mixed my departure time with my time to arrive at the school. I was feeling pretty frustrated upon my arrival at the school.

All these feelings melted away as I stepped into the crowded gymnasium. Children and parents sang Christmas standards in voices that may not have been the best, but were joyous.

Standing there for a moment or two, I started in to singing. It is amazing how it is almost impossible to stay frustrated or angry while singing. My concerns and disappointments melted away to join with the Paxson community in wonderful song.

There were some edits in the songs. I can't remember what they were but I seem to recall that they were probably things that most of the children would not have been able to relate to anyway.

We sang one of my favorite songs which is *The Twelve Days of Christmas*. This is a great song. It deserves its place at any Christmas gathering.

Again, Ms. Callan was there helping to pull off a rousing occasion. It looked like members of the community donated their time to form a band to accompany the children and parents. Good on them.

Well, it seems I don't have room for a general discussion of Christmas. Besides, what hasn't already been said?

Take a little time tomorrow morning if your skies are cloudless to view the partial solar eclipse. It should be good.

Happy Returning

An Observation
Originally published December 26, 2000.

If this day after Christmas is anything like the others I have experienced in my middling existence then you are finding yourself bombarded with advertisements. Welcome to the second biggest shopping day of the year after the day after Thanksgiving.

It is not enough that people have lived an orgiastic shopping frenzy for the last three weeks or so. No, you must spend more because now there will be bargains.

In fact, one major retailer was even advertising after Christmas prices prior to the day itself. How is that for honest desperation?

Like slavering dogs we have been trained to kind of shop before the holiday and then to really let go after Christmas. Could this be the year when the day after Christmas is larger than Thanksgiving plus one? What will their methods have wrought at that point?

One nice aspect of this Christmas was the lack of a runaway toy hit like the Garlic Press Kids or Rummage Me Bilbo. We will be spared any think pieces from media outlets lamenting the selling of our youth and the insanity of their progenitors.

Which reminds me. Why was the Grinch movie so successful? I did not see it but it looked tragically awful like one of the later Batman's in face paint. Wait a minute. Jim Carrey was in one of those, as well. That's it!

I hope you find all the bargains of your heart's content today.

Deregulation-A-Go-Go

A Screed
Originally published December 27, 2000.

When I started this enterprise I pledged that I would work to expose those sorry truths that the media in Montana seems to miss. Whether caused by incompentence or nearsighted boosterism we still need a flashlight of truth in a dark state.

Across our state major industries are shuttering in the face of deregulated electricity prices. Why is this? The popular opinion is that they can no longer afford the power.

Another explanation exists. This is that the companies have purchased long-term electricity contracts. They are safeguarded against the price fluctuations.

Even though they have plenty of power at cheap rates they are closing there doors. Again, why?

These companies have done the math. They can make more money selling their long-term electricity contracts than they can in producing for their industry.

These companies are making the perfectly rational business decision to sell their power and make more money than if they kept their business open and only earned their standard profits. This is American capitalism at its finest. It is not something to lose sleep over.

I am sure that once prices return to former levels these captains of industry will return to productive output. In the mean time they provide some heartburn to the working man, but that should not stand in the way of their search for profits.

There is another explanation. It is that the companies planned poorly and mismanaged their way to having to shutter their businesses.

Uniformity in Action

A Bill Review
Originally published December 28, 2000.

We return to the major-league action of prospective bills before the legislature. Batting clean up is Al Bishop's bill for the mandating of school uniforms in Montana schools.

The bill's language is simple. It makes school officials determine a uniform, set when it is worn, and provide some monetary assistance to the children who might have a hard time purchasing one.

Having worn a school uniform myself for almost a year I feel I have a good handle on this issue. I would say that I am in favor of such a law.

School uniforms combat the effects of

the clothes horse. You all know the type. This person sports every brand name manufactured in several colors and designs and has a seemingly limitless closet.

Furthermore, uniforms fight the hopelessly tasteless. These kids wear shirts colorfully adorned with leaking orifices and vaguely vulgar words. Remove choice from these children's life, please.

Besides, there are those of us who actually liked the looks of girls in uniform. I remember appreciating several. It takes a special person to wear a shapeless shift with aplomb.

There are certainly worse things that could happen to our children than wearing uniforms. Wearing a uniform was something I soon grew accustomed to and enjoyed.

There Goes the Congressperson

A Resignation
Originally published December 29, 2000.

It looks like Montana will not be gaining a return engagement with an additional congressperson. Take a look at the official Census sheet on apportionment.

The numbers reflect Montana's lackluster population production and retention rankings. Our growth rate was again below the national average.

I think some of us are just not doing our part. Are you of reproductive age? You should be having children.

Do you know someone leaving the state? Hide their tickets.

Okay, so these plans will not work. We are really going to experience another ten years as the most populous one-representative state.

There are some advantages to our lowly position. One is that our votes for the electoral college count for much more than, say, Florida's for example. Per person we get a great deal in a presidential race.

It is the other ten years we suffer the indignation of having a single congress flunkie. Let's hope Dennis Rehberg kicks some ass for us.

Montana's Powerless

A Hindsight
Originally published January 1, 2001.

Montana Power Company's hubris has cost their shareholders a bundle. Rarely has a business had such a free hand in its own demise.

As a slight background for the reader new to this issue, Montana Power Company is the corporate paternal twin of Montana's Anaconda Company. It pushed Montana around for almost a century. Montana Power Company had the state legislature write a deregulation bill to their own specifications. Finally, they are selling off their power assets and becoming Touch America, a fiber-optic company.

This is all well and good. Their move to become Touch America looked like a smooth move last year at this time. Most of their revenue was coming from their fiber-optic business. They figured their stock price was deflated because they were considered an electric utility rather than a fixed-line communications company.

By divesting of their power assets they would be able to emulate the vastly overrated stock prices of the telecom firms, thus greatly increasing shareholder value. Life being what happens to your plans, they have instead given their investors a kick in the stomach and displayed faulty business acumen.

Their stock price is a good microcosm of their predicament. Starting 2000 at around $34 they are now around $20. This is actually around the Dow Jones Industry Index average price loss of 40% for fixed-line communications firms. They are well below their market top for the year of $65 set around the end of March.

The ironical part is that those boring old electric utilities are having a heyday in an increasingly uncertain power market. Their stocks represented by the Dow Jones Industry Index for electric utilities are up for the year over 53%. Their stock price could potentially have been sitting at $52 if they had stayed a player in juice.

This brings me back to their lack of market savvy. They wrote the bill to bring deregulation to Montana. If they had waited to sell their assets until now, they would have received much more money. Instead, because they sold their power assets before this hell-for-leather market they got a bad price for their electric assets and they leave their shareholders clutching a greatly devalued telecom firm.

Can someone send Bob Gannon and his staff *The Complete Idiot's Guide to Ruining Your Company?* On second thought, they don't need it.

Montana's Still Powerless

A Further Hindsight
Originally published January 2, 2001.

There is more to add to the Montana Power Company saga. If they had instead sold their fiber-optic business earlier last year, they would have reaped the rewards of a market top in such firms.

As it stands now they are a target for a takeover. With a devalued stock price and a great cash infusion from the sale of assets, you know that some firms are licking their chops to pick up some fiber-optic lines inexpensively.

My guesses for likely suitors include AT&T and Qwest. If either were to be successful, Montana would lose the little base of workers left from MPC.

This is a bittersweet possibility. For while Montana can move forward with the last vestiges of a corporate legacy removed, there could have been another, more constructive way to proceed.

They could have spun off Touch America when that area of the market was on fire. With the money from this stock offering, they could have gone on to become a regional power company player.

This is all speculation now and not terribly productive. Instead, I return to my indictment of the company's management.

Their management philosophy was unsound from the beginning. They grew bored with the power business. In their race away from proven assets and the limits of their knowledge, they followed the siren song of inflated stock values as a corporate strategy.

Stock valuations are what happen as a result of your strategy. They cannot take the place of your strategy.

Martzomania

An Address
Originally published January 3, 2001.

All hail the new governor, Judy Martz. I reckon it is about time I gave her a few words. She deserves them.

First off, I will address her persona. One friend referred to her the other night as "The Church Lady", a character made famous by another Montanan, Dana Carvey. Dana probably based his portrayal on personal experience.

While she does bear a resemblance to Carvey's characterization, she does not seem so benignly kooky. She was sharp enough to mount a successful campaign against Mark O'Keefe's millions. Whether that was credited to her or her advisors, let's give her the benefit of the doubt. She can give as well as she can take.

She strikes me not so much as Marc Racicot's successor as the new Stan Stephens. Although, she seems more in control than Stephens ever did, she has that same unapologetically conservative tone.

A telling example of the secret rift between her and Racicot appeared the other day when Martz tried to redirect tobacco settlement money and was thwarted by Racicot and Mazurek. If they were as palsy-walsy as they have pretended, such an unproductive start to her term would have been avoided.

Unfortunately, a really good read on her political philosophy is unavailable to us. A lieutenant governor does not leave a legacy. She has no other public service record to point to.

However, the glimmers of her personality are beginning to shine through. She is still competitive and strives to win. She may downplay this in a stereotypically feminine fashion but she retains the fighting spirit of the speed skater she was.

Judy Martz is willing to cut corners to further her agenda. This was brought to our attention by her action with the tobacco money. Next time, there will be no check on her.

Grow Your Own

A Bill Review
Originally published January 4, 2001.

It had to happen. We now return to our regularly scheduled roundup of bills before, or somewhat likely to be before the legislature. Our subject today is one of those bills that are rather more likely to not be heard.

Senator Chris Christiaens of Cascade County presents us with the bill draft currently known as LC0039. This bill seeks to allow the commercial farming of hemp.

As interesting a notion as this bill is, it is doomed from the start due to our war on drugs. There is a small portion of the bill toward the bottom that asks for conscientious objector status for Montana. Let's just grow some in peace.

It is not such a radical idea. Hemp has a variety of uses and could be profitable as an alternative crop for our farmers. There is no reasonable person who could deny the above statements.

Canadians are again showing us the error of our ways. Do you drink Canadian whiskey? Ever wonder why? Because they didn't have prohibition. Now, they are growing hemp and loving it.

Will it be any wonder when we have to use Canadian hemp for the next sixty years as our own hemp industry tries to catch up? It will take a braver president than I have lived to see to end the ludicrous aspects of the drug war.

In the mean time bills such as LC0039 will be futile gestures. Futile, yes. Gestures, yes. Sometimes, gestures may presage results.

Besides, if hemp was legalized Montana would probably lose most of the crop to Kentucky and Wisconsin as in years past. We wouldn't have much hemp business anyway.

You Compete Me

A Bill Review
Originally published January 6, 2001.

Could there be more bill reviews? Say it ain't so bad.

Senate Bill 151 seeks to curtail an ever more rapacious university system. Sponsored by Senator Dale Mahlum of Missoula the bill restricts the universities from selling their publicly subsidized wares, specifically their fitness facilities.

This bill confronts the recent trend of our colleges to provide services readily available in our communities. This trend is born of the need for a university to attract students with amenities, to extract as much revenue from students as possible, and to protect students by bringing the outside world to the campus.

Where this trend runs afoul of the community away from campus is that there is competition with businesses. At the University of Montana there was a grocery close to campus called Freddy's Feed and Read. Freddy's is gone now and the University has two convenience stores on either end of campus.

If any other branch of government were to set up so private an industry, citizens would scream. Because it is the University it is excused. Also, after all of the budget cuts the U system has been subjected to, how can we not begrudge them some revenue.

There are no easy answers to this dilemma. I don't think this bill proposes any. It simply stops a campus fitness center from competing with a private gym for the business of non-students.

In the mean time, there are many other venues providing subsidized entertainment to students such as theaters, recreational equipment rental, and libraries.

If we were to provide the level of funding required for our universities, we might be in a better position to have a say in this matter.

Bearing the Costs

A Bill Review
Originally published January 8, 2001.

Water torture by bill review proceeds with an examination of the full costs of government. This bill submitted by Representative Roy Brown of Billings seeks to determine the true costs of certain government services.

By creation of a full cost accounting pilot program for select government agencies, the Republican sponsor hopes to garner some wisdom about the efficiency of government. There is some hope that this system of bookkeeping can shed some light on our public activities. However, there is also doubt that it is as enlightening as it may appear at first glance.

House Bill 73 brings what is termed full cost accounting to a few departments. For those of you scratching your heads about the concept of full cost accounting, it seeks to apportion costs to particular activities.

Let us take mine permitting as an example. Full cost accounting would seek to break down all of the governmental costs of the Department of Environmental Quality as it allows a mine to proceed. Furthermore, these costs would be tracked by job so that one could see how much it costs to license a large mine versus a small mine.

Where this tends to fall apart is that there are many indirect costs shared among many government activities. One would be the electricity used by the department. How should these indirect costs be apportioned across projects? Should all small mines receive the same share as all large mines?

One of the stated objectives of the bill is to ensure, "agency rates and fees for goods and services that are set correctly and fairly." This sounds great. Maybe large mine permittees will need to pay a commensurately larger share of the agency's budget in fees. The opposite argument is that since we all derive benefit from the products of mining we should all shoulder greater costs for those benefits.

Furthermore, don't we all benefit from the clean air and water that our Department of Environmental Quality is responsible for protecting? Do we want them basing a decision on a mine permit because their budget could be affected? Even the appearance of such a case could be counterproductive.

These issues seem to reappear with all departments. One notable exception to the trial departments is the Department of Livestock. Here the costs should be borne by whom? The livestock growers reap the profits. The livestock consumers derive benefits. Vegetarians could plead amnesty but even then they are likely the consumers of numerous by-products.

Public goods are that because their costs and benefits are not easily split.

Stick a Pin in Me

A Bill Review
Originally published January 9, 2001.

      Senator Al Bishop of Billings makes a rare repeat visit to our lowly stage today. You may remember him from his bill to require uniforms in public schools.

      This time he presents us with an attempt to remove automated teller machines from casinos. While this is a noble effort Mr. Bishop does not go far enough.

      The state, in its efforts to get a piece of the action, should sanction automated teller machine gambling. Here's how it would play out.

      A person could gamble with one of their twenties on every transaction. The odds would be a one-in-six chance of winning one hundred dollars with the state collecting every sixth twenty.

This allows the banks to join in the fun. After all, they are usually stuck holding the uncollectible bankruptcies. Why not let them in on the front end?

The state could pay a small transaction fee for each bet. Then, the state could put the proceeds in an account for restitution for prosecuted embezzlement.

I think Al Bishop is definitely on to something here but he is showing the same lack of imagination the other representatives are blighted with. I propose *The Outrider* sponsor a brainstorming session to reveal some truly innovative solutions to the state's problems.

If you have an imaginative method for either raising or spending revenue, contact *The Outrider* at the address below. There could be a prize involved.

Warts and All

A Bill Review
Originally published January 10, 2001.

Who said bill reviews can't be fun? What? Are you crazy?

I do these bill reviews in the hopes that a concerned citizen gets off his ass and participates in our legislative process. Much as I found with the web site reviews, these little snapshots can provide some insights into our state of Montana.

Whether they are excessively boring, and some are, I assure you. Or, whether you have to change your undies on completion, these simple expositions can help provide an understanding of our legislature.

I am certain it is in the same spirit that Republican Representative Mark Noennig of Billings proposes House Bill 144. This bill seeks to provide C-Span-like coverage of the Montana legislature.

While our lawmakers probably strike you as a boring set, I believe there are some roses among the onions. Watching gavel-to-gavel coverage should confirm this.

Let us hope the legislature finds the available funding. It is expensive, but it will be worth it.

As much as we can encourage the involvement of our citizens, the better our government will be.

Et Tu, Schneider?

A Different Kind of Bill Review
Originally published January 11, 2001.

This Sunday in a certain local Montana paper an editorial was printed by Bill Schneider, the former owner of Falcon Press. For those of you having missed this editorial he said Montana needed to do four things to ensure economic growth.

First, Montana needs to weaken employee protections. This would help convince employers to move here. Secondly, Montana should lower its income tax because highly paid executives would never make the decision to move here because our income taxes are too high.

Thirdly, bring back airline re-regulation to boost up a sad flight situation. Fourthly, preserve our clean environment.

I guess there is a little there for both Democrats and Republicans to hate. Why did I find his opinions so ridiculous?

Making Montana out to be some scheming employee heaven is absurd. I am sure all of the employees laid off this year would agree. His own former nameplate had no problem eliminating 50 jobs in Montana.

Income taxes are never the full story. Our tax rate is one of the highest in the country. However, our tax burden on each citizen is about average. If taxes were the culprit, Connecticut's economy should be near the bottom with an average tax burden roughly double ours.

He didn't make much of a case for airline re-regulation. I don't know if he could. I feel like we have pretty decent service and pricing for our location. Maybe I am in the minority. I doubt the government will do better by us. I'll stick with Carter on this decision.

Finally, preservation of our wilderness and natural assets should be a priority. Even with this, we can continue to have a vital natural resources portion of our economy. Perhaps, he was just ignoring this.

All four of these issues are really on the side of the chief reasons we have a hard time attracting industries. I'll address the true four issues in tomorrow's *Outrider*.

Economic Development 101

A Lesson
Originally published January 12, 2001.

In yesterday's column I tore Bill Schneider a new one over his asinine opinions about economic development. I said I would try to set the record straight about what it takes to promote economic development. It ain't missile logic.

There are four basic issues a company considers when deciding to move to a location. The first is proximity to markets.

A bread company wants to locate by bread eaters so that it is easy and inexpensive to move the bread to the eaters.

The second issue is availability of labor. Is there a large enough labor pool to keep recruitment and retention costs low?

The first two factors mitigate against Montana. We are isolated from population centers and are not a population center ourselves. There is no getting around the fact that we have a hard time competing with more populous areas.

The third factor a company will consider is the closeness of manufacturing resources. These may be raw materials. These may also be support industries. Take Silicon Valley. There are numerous ancillary companies allowing the main companies to succeed. These pilot fish become acquainted with the peculiarities of the industry and are able to spread their knowledge to other manufacturers.

The fourth concern of a relocating company is the package offered by a government in the form of incentives and tax breaks. All other things being equal this fourth element can make a difference.

Montana's government can contribute by recruiting businesses with packages of government largesse. We can also inventory the resources we have available to offer interested movers.

These two simple things can help to move us out of our economic doldrums. I know our government has taken steps to do these in the past. A few more resources to these efforts in an ongoing fashion will yield incredible results.

Jesse and Me

A Remembrance
Originally published January 15, 2001.

One of Martin Luther King's assistants was Jesse Jackson. The Reverend Jesse Jackson has become one of the most visible leaders of the African-American community. This is a brief story of my experience with Mr. Jackson.

In 1984, Jesse Jackson ran for president for the first time. His message of economic assistance to the less fortunate and racial harmony caught fire with enough Democratic voters to spawn an even more successful run in 1988.

I joined his campaign in 1984 in New Hampshire as a volunteer. I drove the writing press in his motorcade. I squired such luminaries as Jack White from *Time* and

Sylvester Monroe of *Newsweek*.

At one time I even drove the "death van". This van had equipment that the network crews would use to broadcast live in the case of the candidate being shot. This was a realistic concern as Jackson had numerous death threats phoned in against him and was given a large Secret Service detail as a precaution.

I don't have many anecdotes about Jackson as I never met him in New Hampshire. I figured that he should meet me. I was volunteering for him, after all.

Truth be told. Jesse Jackson is an aloof figure. He saw me driving his motorcade numerous times and did not stop to introduce himself to a young, idealistic staffer. If you think the staff was so large it was overwhelming, you would be wrong. There were about ten core members of which I was one.

This might be the reason that Jackson has never been able to achieve the pinnacle of political or inspirational success. He lacks the common touch so necessary if one is to lead so many.

I did eventually meet the man in 1988 in Arlee. I stood at a rope line and shook his hand.

Tooting the Horn

A Boast
Originally published January 16, 2001.

Over three months of *The Outrider* have come and gone. I thought it was well on time to discuss our successes.

Way back at the beginning, who would have thought that web site reviews of the candidates would prove so enlightening. Surely, not any other news outlet. Who knew that a School Superintendent candidate threatening death could barely spell herself? You heard it here people.

Whether it proved to be humorous or not, the fact that Dennis Rehberg was able to keep his site updated and Nancy Keenan allowed hers to languish was a signal that he took his race seriously. The fact that Karla Gray answered my e-mail proved that she was more responsive than many of the candidates who would not accept an e-mail from me.

Moving on to the post election highlights, we covered Marc Racicot's chad debacle from beginning to bork. I don't know if he reads us but he would have been considerably less surprised as we scooped all other forms of media in predicting that a seat in Bush's cabinet would not be his.

Looking at personal favorites I have to mention our Return to Denver series. Whether the massacre at Columbine touched your family directly or not, it provides a lesson in loving our children and building a better world.

Finally, we are providing a service in reviewing bills before the legislature. These have the power to affect your future for years to come. Our coverage has consistently topped anything available anywhere, any time.

Prepare your mind folks. This has only been the beginning.

On sabbatical until February.

R & R Report

A Libation
Originally published Febuary 5, 2001.

A much deserved rest was had by this writer and editor. I went to the American forefathers ancestral tidelands to glean some substance of the heartbreak and love that combined to create our land.

Before I pour you a cup of reminiscence let me say that my article about Jesse Jackson was intended to take advantage of the Martin Luther King holiday not his recent misfortunes. Way back in 1984 Jesse displayed a knack for great hypocrisy as evidenced by the "Hymietown incident" wherein he slurred Jews even as he strove to build a rainbow coalition.

The first English colonists to build a permanent settlement embarked off the

James river at a site they called Jamestown. Thought lost to the seas, the remains of the original fort were only recently discovered in 1995. This was thanks to some Virginia ladies who at the turn of the 20th century acted to purchase land to assist preservation.

Walking that ground where so many of the colonists gave up their lives to disease, hunger, and cold, I had the feeling that the establishment of English settlement was no Disney movie. For the Native Americans as well, could they foresee the wasting of their lives in the sufferings and deprivations of these strangers?

At the other end of the peninsula I spent a worthy two days at America's hallowed ground of freedom, Yorktown. This was the location of the decisive battle of the revolution.

I had always thought the battle was fought by infantry in an open field. The actual battle was a siege in which artillery was the critical element of victory. Cut off by sea, once the siege lines had been extended to permit cannonading of Yorktown, the British had no choice but to surrender.

With the capitulation of Cornwallis' army, the revolution was won and we had gained our freedom. Here's to the patriots, pioneers, and previous inhabitants who blazed the trail. May we make them proud.

Shet Mah Mouth

A Scowl
Originally published February 6, 2001.

What should greet my wondering eyes and ears on my return to Montana? Is it the governor pushing an economic development plan? The legislature seeking solutions to rising energy prices? None of the above?

It seems the governor is more concerned with celebrating her victory in February. The legislature is basking in silence, as well.

With almost a third of the 2001 legislature behind us, the GOP seem stunned into inaction. Perhaps, their unprecedented reign at the helm of Montana is spooking them. I don't have an explanation.

I did have an expectation. Okay,

maybe a couple or more. They are not being met. Where is the stimulus for the economy? Where is help with electricity deregulation in the face of California's colossal failure?

I'm ready to declare the honeymoon over for both our new governor and the legislature. They need to get to work.

Granted the solutions to the economy should be right up the GOP's alley. They have no excuse for not comprehending the economic realities of growing our economy. The tougher pill to swallow may be that avoiding the deregulation issue makes any action on development an uphill struggle.

Perhaps, they are practicing the strategy of doing nothing. In this, they are succeeding.

The Raser's Edge

A Bill Review
Originally published February 7, 2001.

How could it be that we are returning to a bill review? Did we do something bad in a previous lifetime? Unfortunately, none of that matters. We go forward.

Holly Raser, Democrat of Missoula, submits House Bill 356 which seeks to require a vote for any size of annexation. Currently, for annexations of less than 300 parcels no vote of the annexed is required but the action can still be overturned via petition.

On the surface, a bill of this nature does not seem to make much of a difference either way. A petition can perform the same function as an election.

However, small questions such as this form the basis of our democracy. Also, the cost and time involved will be borne either by the citizens directly affected or of the taxpayers of the entity wishing to do the annexation.

I think this bill is a good idea. If a little democracy is good, why not a little more?

This simply codifies rights which citizens should have the option of exercising no matter the size of the annexation. It prevents cities from stringing together small annexation areas to avoid a vote, and it encourages participation from those exurbanites.

Finally, it puts the financial burden upon the taxpayers of the government which is seeking advantage through an incorporation.

Howard's End

A Television Review
Originally published February 8, 2001.

I watched the television show *Joseph Kinsey Howard, A Life Outside the Margins* on KUFM public television last night. I wish I could say I enjoyed it more than I did.

While the special had interviews with contemporaries and friends, historians and journalists, as well as taped material from Mr. Howard's lifetime the production values were distracting enough to warrant a poor review.

In particular, the clunky use of sound effects was much more grating than gratifying. The panning of poorly lit newpaper clippings was also annoying.

Rather than emphasizing his inspiring words, the production had a rushed feeling that swallowed his important ideas in stock footage and life details.

Surely, someone who is considered a great Montanan could provide an inspirational portrait. Instead, we were told often and again of his greatness without experiencing it for ourselves.

The simple chronological structure of the presentation made what could have been stimulating, tendentious. Perhaps, the use of a voice-over of quotes from Howard would have helped us gather his power. Instead, I can't think of a really important thing Howard said.

This production did not need to be so straightforward. If it had used some slightly more advanced documentary techniques it could have illustrated the man for our enlightenment.

Get Lost, Marc!

A Good Riddance
Originally published February 9, 2001.

I know I have covered this ground to some small extent in the past. I simply feel that it is time to extend a finger to one of Montana's worst governors of our contemporary era.

Again, I find the parallels between Monsieur Racicot and Mister Clinton too obvious to ignore. Both squandered times of prosperity and good feelings in the pursuit of...what? Popularity?

Both Racicot and Clinton decided early in their first terms that they really did not want to accomplish anything but retaining the chair they sat in. To this end, they both geared down any ambitions they may have had to lead, and chose to lounge.

This is the crime I will indict them both of, Failure to Stand for Anything. It did not have to be this way.

They were certainly both accomplished deceivers and scoundrels. I know there were quite a few people who thought that they would try to carry through on their initial proposals. Once fooled, apparently these same folks found themselves gladdened by the boosting economy and forgot rhetoric to embrace the dollar.

With the major failures of utility deregulation and economic development coming in to sharp relief as Monsieur Racicot takes his leave, I have no choice but to hold him largely responsible for the state of our affairs. He was not the driver, but he never spoke up as his party's car ran us over.

So it is with a glad heart I wave my single-fingered salute to Monsieur Racicot. May we not see your kind again.

Lincoln's Birthday

A Meditation
Originally published February 12, 2001.

Abraham Lincoln was a most unusual president. He was no warrior, however, he found the strength to lead the country in its most devastating war.

Lincoln was also unusual in not having come from money like almost all of our other great presidents: Washington, Jefferson, and the two Roosevelts. He had to maintain a career until his election to the presidency to keep his head above water.

Also, singular among the top five to die in office from an assassin's bullet. You could make the case that he was hated by more than half of the country when he died.

All of this he earned for giving his life

in his stance for the principle of the protection of the minority from the tyranny of the majority. A precept we continue to struggle with even today.

The Civil War did not solve this issue, although it could be said that it made those proponents of intolerance work to conceal their true aims. In Montana, we are rarely confronted by hatred displayed with open abandon.

It saddens me that this underground abusive fringe is still with us. I can't help but think that Mr. Lincoln would try to end their days.

I would like to ask you to speak out against unkindness and violence when you see it. Let's make our society a civil one.

Big Box of Shame

A Rant
Originally published February 13, 2001.

Passing by a Wal-Mart Hyper-Duper Spasmo SuperMart under construction in the Clark Fork valley, I could not help but be disgusted by the almost complete lack of aesthetic consideration by the architect. Does a giant box structure such as this even require an architect?

If there was an architect, he was probably paid for one design and the Wal-Mart corporation has built 1,000 stores from this single misapplication of design. I'm letting the architect off the hook right now. He was probably uninspired and in need of the money. He may have even known of the foul purposes Wal-Mart would put his design to, but he had a family to feed.

No, the blame for this eyesore rests with triangular precision upon the Wal-Mart corporation. While they are not the only perpetrators of visual blight, they are certainly one of the most obvious.

Even as they build a huge box down by our beautiful river they were tacking a couple of peaked roof towers to the side of the temple of commerce. It is almost as if the shame of their artistic crime caused them to grab even the slightest of architectural emollients.

Wal-Mart is so obviously displaying contempt for any expense that could bring a gratifying loveliness to their locale. Perhaps, Wal-Mart is an uglifactor of great wealth, to borrow from Theodore Roosevelt.

I have a simple solution to this problem. Provide a law that all corporate executives of Wal-Mart must be buried in caskets resembling their own stores.

We might eventually have a situation where a Wal-Mart store looks like a half-decent sepulcher. It could only be an improvement.

Genuine Junk

A Review
Originally published February 14, 2001.

    Local Missoula, Western Montana, Continental Dividers; Cash for Junkers; a musical band, has released their first recorded collection of music titled *Genuine Junk*. I caught their act tonight as sponsored by the local college radio station, KBGA, with their *Live in Missoula* free concert series at the University of Montana.

  A rollicking country and blues band they smoked the stage and thoroughly entertained the small audience in attendance at the UC theatre. A local standard, they have a polished, highly professional sound that if there is any justice in this world will be appreciated by country music fans across the globe.

A tight ensemble of six players, they manage to pack their sound with pedal steel, mandolin, fiddle, and numerous guitars played to perfection. Spare numbers allow full experimentation by the ensemble with folk roots laid bare.

I must admit I have been a fan of theirs for some time. They used to have a regular Sunday night appearance at Charlie's, a Missoula watering hole.

When they played Charlie's in the narrow corridor which barely passes for a stage and yet provides no elevation for its players they squished themselves into that arena and gave it full heart. I might be mistaken but it seems they have blossomed as songwriters in the intervening time.

While keeping to the standbys of love and loss, their music did not lack for whiskey, regret, and smoking. All right, perhaps their songs didn't set me on fire lyrically, however, they seemed vastly appropriate.

Please, look for the Cash for Junkers CD in your town. I think you will be glad that you did.

Have Faith

A Spew
Originally published February 15, 2001.

I read an editorial yesterday in the *Wall Street Journal* written by John J. DiIulio Jr. the new head of President Bush's White House Office of Faith-Based and Community Initiatives. The article did not discuss his job history so I do not have much background on the man. I guess that does not matter so much as his noxious views.

His supposition is that this newly created office should have three goals. These are: to augment charitable giving, to end discrimination against religious providers of social services, and to mobilize support for grassroots groups, both religious and secular.

All three of these goals are misguided

and at their heart undemocratic. I have previously espoused how I think President Bush is making an end run around our democracy to promote state-sponsored religion. Let me write today about the mistaken beliefs leading to Mr. DiIulio Jr.'s goals.

Charitable giving should be just that, charitable giving. If the fund-raisers of a particular cause are not successful, let me assure you there is a better person willing to help secure donations just beyond the church wall. The country's tax revenue represents a sweet and easy victory pot to exploit for religious purposes.

The money raised from taxes should not go to religious groups. The individual's decision to provide money to religious groups of their own interest should rule supreme.

By Mr. DiIulio Jr.'s second goal one might suppose there is a problem with discrimination against religious providers of social services. This is obviously one of those problems that was so widespread and pernicious that it completely escaped my notice.

As for his third goal of mobilizing grassroots support, I think the federal government and the grassroots are a contradiction in terms. Rather than trying to build one with the other he would be better pressed to learn the difference.

I know I have made light of these issues. However, I want you to know, dear reader, that I do not take this assault on our democracy lightly. I am speaking up about these conditions for oppression in hopes of bringing their halt.

Dry Me a River

An Observation
Originally published February 16, 2001.

It is that time again in Montana. Every politician performs a small play meant for public consumption. Yes, you guessed it. It is time for the drought pronouncements.

Those of you who have not observed Montana for any length may suppose that these pronouncements are serious and dire. You might conclude that drought is inevitable and likely to be severe.

Let me ease your fears. This is the time of year when every politician polishes off their yearly drought pronouncement.

You see, this is the perfect time to speak about drought. Winter could soon prove your drought pronouncement wrong, so you try to get ahead of the moisture and say that the conditions are ripe for drought.

You convey your serious intent with an oh-so-serious look upon your face. The farmers, ranchers, timber interests, etcetera, should be aware that drought is heading our way. The snowpack is down this year.

Now, for those of you with primarily flatland experience a low snowpack sounds as serious as a hurricane. The truth be told it is only an average and in February the wettest months of the year are still to come in Montana. There is plenty of time for recovery.

However, politicians realize that the time to make political hay from a supposed drought could vanish as rapidly as the next blizzard. So, they all rush out during February with their serious looks and speeches.

Take it all with a grain of dust. The chances of a drought are really made in May and June.

Belated Valentine

A Pæan
Originally published February 20, 2001.

Here is to love and lovers wherever they may be. What is love but the life force that propels all of us on?

There are two countervailing forces in the universe. One is love and the other hate. One is life and one is death.

Love=life Hate=death

They may not be exact equivalents but I think it is true.
Here on our wondrous globe the force of love and life is strongest. Oh, hate and death have had their days. But it is obvious to me that love is winning out.

Another rough pair of equivalents

could be that love is order and hate is chaos. Life is organized by DNA, society, and family. Death is disintegration and entropy.

One extremely valid scientific principle is that of entropy. This states that systems will move toward chaos.

Science is at a loss to explain why our world would be so organized and incredibly varied in life. Science is often at a loss as to why the most important elements of our life occur.

The answer to these questions is profoundly beyond science. That is my belief anyway.

However, it can be known by any young lover. Go find out for yourself.

Letter from the Editor

A Complaint
Originally published February 23, 2001.

You may have noticed a lack of consistency this past week. I must confess to being at a loss for words.

I started this seed of a newsmagazine to cover the imponderables and unimagined aspects of Montana's wealth of diversity. Unfortunately, I find Montana stuck in such an incredible rut it is depressing me.

You could have written the stories about the legislature in any of the last six years of biennial sessions. Lawmakers weakening environmental laws as a means of economic development.

The true causes of economic development left relatively undisturbed. Our state's balance between labor and business shifting further to the right.

I keep looking for some leadership. Unfortunately, at the state level we seem bereft.

And, all of this is happening while a profound disruption in our energy pricing is occurring. It is too depressing for words frankly.

He Keeps Going and Going

A Notice and Speculation
Originally published March 12, 2001.

Just when you think you have written everything. When you have grown despondent over the ludicrous state of affairs. The ridiculous occurs to raise that last little bit of ire. Don't lose that ire. Protect that ire.

Like the bad penny of legend our somewhat esteemed former governor has reemerged as a media figure. It seems the private sector is simply too small to contain our old leader.

What could have convinced the chadmeister to leave his new law firm for even a moment? It would have to be the convincing proof that Florida's butterfly ballot was a cause in throwing the election to Bush.

Now, I think Mr. Bush is president and I don't suppose we should endlessly rehash the election spectacle. At the same time, the idea that the butterfly ballot provoked confusion in significant enough numbers to cost Gore the election seems well-founded. It is a pity that such a critical error could not have been the basis for any kind of an electoral challenge.

Described variously as a vocal Bush supporter or a Republican spokesman, Citizen Racicot dismissed the findings of the *Palm Beach Post* as "science fiction". Sounding like a scientist himself he used such phrases as: "There seems to be a disparity in the analysis," "The basis upon which you draw a conclusion is subject to incredible impeachment," and "You're trying too hard to find a correlation here."

He seems to have a healthy respect for the scientific method since the asbestos frosting of his hometown escaped his notice. Perhaps, only particles larger than a chad rate his penetrating analysis.

But, Racicot's further time in the limelight (it is Florida, after all) is to what demi-evil purpose? There has been supposition in these quarters that Comrade Racicot was jettisoned by Bush. Could there be a different scenario?

Cheney's bum ticker is getting worse by the day. The Bush team knew after his fourth heart attack that Big Dick might have to lay off the White House beat.

Why not create a replacement in Monsieur Racicot? Concoct a cover story about him turning down the Attorney General slot. Wait a few months to prevent the Cheney resignation from ruining the honeymoon and then nominate Lord Racicot to replace the failing Cheney.

Although Herr Racicot was adamant that he never sought a quid pro quo in his advocacy of a Bush administration, what is he still doing fighting the lame fight after he made such a show of hastening to the private sector? If he doesn't have a deal, I, at least, hope he is getting paid.

Letter from the Editor

A Review of Views
Originally published March 19, 2001.

I've been thinking of changing our update statement to "updated very weakly". However, I sincerely hope to keep up with interesting events in Montana and celebrate them with you.

Perhaps, I am not cut out for the news gathering business. I seem to be so bored by most of the happenings in Montana. Are there some fascinating things happening out there? If so, I might portray them.

Truthfully, putting this site together in my spare time has been somewhat taxing. Also, I am finding myself at a loss as to content.

I've vented some spleen and it was fun

but now I don't wish to repeat myself if I am not adding something clever and original.

The situation could change. I might find out some dreadful facts in the next several days and write an interesting column about it.

In other words, I am more than likely hanging up my spurs. It has been a time. A wonderful and fun time. Maybe, I should even find a little free web space to park my archives. The main Outrider site will probably close.

Thank you, dear reader. Don't give up the hope that Montana will grow up and get serious about its place in the world.

Letter from the Editor

A Return to the Barbed Edge
Originally published May 23, 2001.

      After a slightly extended sabbatical, a well needed one at that, I am back to give you all the business. If there is anything worse than hanging around, it is facing up to the pathetic choices for media I have. Besides, I fascinate me.

      Along with the painful relics I consume are the stories that scream for *The Outrider* touch. I think if you developed the love of this site that I did, you may know of what I speak.

      A potent reminder occurred the other night as I was watching the tenth anniversary of *Backroads of Montana*. Maybe listening to all the white males of Montana Public Television made me think there has to be some more options out there for the loving consumer of Montana media.

Maybe it was seeing a commercial, or was it an endorsement, for the same public television and hearing one of Montana's many white male editors saying how much they valued public television.

Now, I do not pretend I am not another white male editor. However, I am aware of the strides we need to make to allow the voices of the minority representation.

So, sit back and enjoy as I stick my fingers up your nose. *The Outrider* has returned from journeys ahead of the herd.

Flipping the Flops

One man makes a compassionate stand.
Originally published May 25, 2001.

        Senator James Jeffords decided to take Bush at his compassionate words. Unfortunately for Bush, he is as craven and cynical as Clinton ever was.

        The Republicans wanted Bush to be their Clinton. Now, he is. And, they are paying the price.

        It is fine to take Senator Jeffords at his words and give him the benefit of the doubt that his decision is one of conscience. I can't help noting that, perhaps, he felt that benefits only could be accrued before Strom Thurmond's likely demise.

        Our dim bulb Senator Burns said that this will not change the situation in the Senate. Perhaps, he should repeat civics. Of course, he is simply parroting the party line that everything is fine.

With Baucus' hard-won seniority coming into play, Montana should be prepared for a wealth of spoils in the months ahead. Even Burns can coast on that.

I don't see how anyone can not recognize a major blow to the Bush presidency. Also, an incredible victory for the Senate Democrats that November had left in the air.

Big Brother is Eavesdropping

A International News Review
Originally published May 29, 2001.

Listening to the BBC at noon on Montana Public Radio I heard a story about how members of the European Parliament are recommending all e-mail senders in Europe encrypt their communications because the United States is surveilling all forms of communication in Europe and around the world.

This caused me to look up the story on the BBC News web site. It seems that Europe has valid reasons to be concerned that the United States; acting in concert with Canada, Australia, the United Kingdom, and New Zealand, is intercepting a vast amount of critical communication data.

While I do not doubt that this spying is

taking place and I found the further back story fascinating, including the idea that Europe believes the U.S. is using this information to win commercial bids, I think the silence of the American media on this story is more incredible.

Just to see if the media quietude was real or imagined I looked at my two favorite news web sites. In the world section of cnn.com there was no headline. I was able to search on the word "echelon", the name of the secret project, and found a similar story to the BBC's. It was hidden but at least it was accessible.

Unfortunately, the world section of abcnews.com did not yield any such story. Not only was it not a headline, it was not found with a search.

Perhaps, their editors decided it was not newsworthy. However, let us think of the reverse situation. If another country was found to be spying on every e-mail in our nation, wouldn't that be a headline. Of course, it would. Read the headlines that made it on to this site in its place. I am sure you can find a funny one.

We are Martzing to Utopia

A Scourge to Your Mother
Originally published May 31, 2001.

I have been pretty silent about Judy Martz. Perhaps, her inability to get a mention in these parts is the reason she fired her communications team.

As much as I would love to believe that scenario, the reason for my silence on Granny Martz is that she hasn't merited any attention. In fact, it is this conspicuous languishment that is the impetus for this column.

In a favorable circumstance, an incoming governor has the ninety days of their first biennial session to really impress the state with their platform and ideas. After that, well...who knows?

Crone Martz had the most favorable of circumstances, both houses of the Montana legislature run by the Republicans. Yet, she was silent.

Did she not want to accomplish anything? Did she care? These are questions I have pondered. I can't come up with much. However, the evidence of her inaction is clear.

With economic development and electricity deregulation needing attention, she checked out. Now, she is firing the messengers of her lethargy. Look in the mirror, lotus-eater.

PSC Correct

A Nail in Their Side
Originally published June 1, 2001.

Rather than roll over and take it from the DeRepublicans, the PSC wisely is staking its own claim to a safer energy future for the public. The PSC grew a spine apparently and decided that they do have the power the citizens invested in them to protect ratepayers.

For much of the entire energy debate the PSC has been a sideline observer, never very certain of its strength. This declaration reflects the knowledge of their public trust.

In what was a startling show of solidarity it seems they have reached agreement on their ability to use sweeping measures, including regulating rates, to tame a hostile utility environment. This is exactly what the situation needs.

The creators of the present Montana government certainly appear wise in their granting of separate powers to a Public Service Commission. And, this wisdom is evident in the commission's reaction to one-party rule for over a decade. The commission is acting in a bipartisan manner to protect consumers.

The legislature left one task undone in their run to deregulate, and that was to deactivate the people's utility representatives. This situation could be likened to the state loosing higher education and failing to eliminate the Board of Regents.

In the vacuum of legislative and gubernatorial leadership, the Public Service Commissioners receive this editor's profiles in political courage award.

Wet and Wild

An Observation
Originally published June 4, 2001.

With Montana's media drifting towards the sensational every day, one would think we are experiencing the worst drought conditions ever imagined. Frankly, it is bad in some parts.

In fact, President Bush went ahead and declared us drought stricken so our attachment to the federal breast is secure for this year. Trouble is, what if you have a drought and it rains on your parade?

I have previously taken politicians to task for their pandering. I think it is only fair I give the media its share of blame.

While things have been dry, it is no secret that June is the wettest month of the year. It seems like jumping the gun to cry dry when we haven't even given rain a chance.

Furthermore, the media love weather news. They love to sensationalize adverse weather conditions. This happens to a huge degree in other areas.

I have been caught in a media frenzy for Hurricane Fran and a huge blizzard in Manhattan. On both occasions, the actual weather was considerably less than advertised. Fran drizzed rain on Charleston and it snowed a few inches in Manhattan.

On both occasions media coverage was out of all bounds for both events. This is what I am seeing for the drought.

Weather news is great for the media because it is the only topic that they can report on that is not in some way controversial. And, since controversy loses advertisers, weather is their only sure revenue generator.

Lies, Damn Lies, and Statistics

Behind the Numbers
Originally published June 6, 2001.

I recently read in a local newspaper, which shall remain nameless, a piece about HIV/AIDS statistics in the state. There were said to be 522 total cases in the state. Also, 89 new cases added in the year 2001.

Knowing that the Montana Department of Public Health and Human Services had been keeping these statistics for years I saw the 89 new cases as a huge jump in the rate of transmission. I traveled over to their web site and saw that these infection numbers were kept since 1985.

Was Montana in the midst of an epidemic? Actually it turns out to not be the case.

Jim Murphy of the Communicable Disease Program explained that they had simply changed their accounting methods to include people who had HIV yet had never displayed AIDS symptoms. This single jump of 74 HIV cases will not be repeated.

Take a look at this report for yourself. You might even notice that the total cases are actually 526, not 522, as reported by the above nameless paper.

But this story is not about poor fact checking. Nor, is it about the lack of context for an unusual statistical item. Although, both existed.

It is about the hidden truth that lies in a simple number.

Goin' Clayzy

A Celebration
Originally published June 15, 2001.

Although I am not about to turn fifty, have only a passing interest in clay, and do not play host to a gypsy band of artists every year. The same cannot be said of the Archie Bray Foundation in Helena. Art museums statewide are helping the Bray, as it is known in Helena, celebrate its first fifty years.

If you are the kind of person who loves to get in on ground zero of a party of this magnitude, I highly recommend being in Helena next week. You can get all the party details and plan accordingly. Some events are already sold out, so you better hurry.

For a lovely dilettante weekend how could you beat the auction on Friday, June 22 and the Brickyard Bash on Saturday, June 23?

The Brickyard Bash is one of the best dances in Helena and the state and is much anticipated by fans of the Big Sky Mudflaps.

Of course, how could I leave out the activities of the Holter Museum of Art? They have been working on this fete, as well. Attend a special member's preview of an exhibit toasting the Bray tonight.

The Holter is also publishing a book lauding the Bray's first 50 in conjunction with its Ceramic Continuum exhibition.

However, you don't have to live or visit Helena to get a taste of the Bray. The Art Museum of Missoula is breaking out its own exhibit on Rudy Autio. The opening is today from 5 to 8.

And, in what is billed as a statewide occasion, even the Yellowstone Art Museum is showing its clay collection. I think you should take a look at your local arts house for a peep at how they are saluting a noble Montana institution. Happy Birthday, Bray!

Political Postmortem

A Case Study
Originally published June 18, 2001.

How does a candidate who outspends his opponent, a relative political neophyte, three-to-one end up losing the race for the governor's chair? Strange as it may seem, Mark O'Keefe accomplished this task in the year 2000.

Before I start my analysis I will also say what I am leaving out of this mix. I will not assume that Montana is an all Republican state. Although a good case can be made, I prefer to consider this a race fought on fair ground.

Also, I will disregard all rumors emanating from Helena, especially about a cocky O'Keefe team burning bridges with other democratic operatives in the primary.

No, I want to stick to the facts as clearly available to the public.

There was the politically suicidal statement by Mr. O'Keefe that he would be industry's "worst nightmare". As bad as this was, and I give him the benefit of the doubt that he was being jocular, even worse was his reaction when this phrase was used against him in a campaign by the largest industries to aid Judy Martz.

He should have known this phrase was damaging and prepared a commercial with the following script:

O'Keefe: You may have heard that I said I would be industry's worst nightmare. I was just joking about that. If I was being serious, I would have said I would be a bad industry's worst nightmare, or a polluter's worst nightmare. I take Montana very seriously, and if some corporation wants to come here and despoil our great land they will have to get past me.

The industry ad campaign hammered at the nightmare phrase with no response from O'Keefe. I believe it is widely known in political circles that you need to respond rapidly to such negative information. Why no answer from O'Keefe?

In what was also a misfire, O'Keefe did not use the cover of this industry ad campaign to pump more money into his race. Instead, he struck a course of sneakily injecting funds at the last minute.

If he had simply said at some point, "Yes, I have a lot of money at my disposal and I am going to use it to win this race because it is very important to me and the people of Montana," he might have confronted an issue that did not serve him well in his efforts to appear aboveboard.

Oh yes, and his opponent ran a campaign without such mistakes.

Punchin' Judy

A "Get the Hell Out" Call
Originally published December 10, 2001.

Sad days for Montana when we return to an utterly corrupt administration, a bought and paid for legislature, and a lapdog media. In my schooling I learned that these features of Montana were ills of our sad corporate history. How eye-opening to return to this time!

Let's start with the most egregious symptom of corpocracy, our Governor Judy Martz is convicted in this quarter of bribe-taking. She gains a piece of land by paying below its true worth. Sounds like a good deal, except when the briber is Sandy Stash and the Arco corporation. Ms. Stash and Arco are subject to regulation by the state and as such have an obligation to stick to legal forms of bribery, such as campaign contribution.

And, how does Judy Martz explain her position. She says that she and Sandy are friends. Oh! that makes it all OK Judy! Go back to being governor now.

Also, Judy says that she and her husband really, really wanted the land for a long time. These explanations display nothing so much as Judy's stupidity.

I have a solution, though. It is simple. It can be accomplished tomorrow. Judy should resign.

She no longer has anyone's trust. She is the most ineffective governor I have seen in my lifetime. She might as well make it easy on the state and get the hell out!

That she avoided prosecution for this misdeed by keeping it a secret beyond the statute of limitations is no excuse for being allowed to remain in an office of public trust.

There have been suggestions in some quarters that she should simply pay back the difference in the land's value as a beginning to regaining trust. I know of no other corruption that is as easily forgiven. Let me state again, she shouldn't pay back, she should get out.

While I am examining this issue, I think the state should call for a replacement to Sandy Stash in its dealing with Arco. Ms. Stash is as guilty as her shill.

Judy, I gave you the benefit of the doubt. You proved to be unworthy of that trust. Good-bye!

The Get Along Gang

Who Are These People And Where Are Their Ethics?
Originally published December 11, 2001.

Why is there no cry for Disgraceful Judy to depart from her unnatural throne? Where are the Democrats? Surely they ought to be able to raise a cry of resignation.

Is it because they cannot imagine any candidate, Karl Ohs in particular, being easier to shellac in 2004 than Judy? Shame on them for putting political expediency before the state's welfare.

What about her own party? I am certainly not letting the Republicans off the hook for Judy's behavior. They should be in the forefront of calling for her removal. After all, one should keep their own house in order.

How about her fellow governors? A

group of western governors, albeit heavily Republican, recently elected Judy to a leadership post. What were they thinking?

In one of Judy's statements she explained that she told former governor Racicot about her land deal. Where are Racicot's words of condemnation? It makes me wonder if this is simply the tip of some shady iceberg for his administration.

Our state constantly frets about economic development. How about social development? How about removing corruption from the highest office in our fair land?

Susan Egan

A Musical Review
Originally published December 13, 2001.

A couple of weeks ago I had the sublime pleasure of hearing live, in person, one of my idols, Susan Egan. For those of you unfamiliar with her song stylings, she played opposite an animated Hercules for Disney.

She was in town to sing show and Christmas tunes with the Missoula Symphony. What a delight! And the symphony sounded wonderful itself. She complimented them twice in what I assume was all sincerity.

She was selling and signing copies of her first solo CD, *all that & more*, and donating some of the proceeds to the symphony. A solo CD for such an incredible talent is long overdue, I am sure.

While I didn't finagle an interview, I have been listening to the album relentlessly and declare it superb. Ms. Egan's voice is astonishing but I think what sets her apart is her ability to fully inhabit the character of the part she is singing. She is so believable.

Whether as the vampy Meg in Hercules or the simpering high school girl in the song, Joshua Noveck, she sells it baby and I will buy it all day long.

For the recording she includes mostly previously performed show songs. These include the marvelously wafting Little Dream and a great syncopated duet with Guy Haines from *Damn Yankees* of Two Lost Souls.

I consider myself lucky to have had a chance to see her in person and purchase an autographed CD of her work. Do not miss Susan Egan if she comes to your town.

Lynch Him!

A Movie Critique
Originally published December 17, 2001.

           David Lynch's newest movie *Mulholland Drive* finally opened in Missoula at the Wilma. This brings to four the films of the native Missoula son I have seen at the grandest theatre of the town of his birth.

    While two were relatively straightforward tales, *Dune* and *The Straight Story. Blue Velvet* and *Mulholland Dr.* were more free-flowing and symbolic. I would have to say that this effort would be roughly comparable to *Blue Velvet* in terms of tone and plot.

    My favorites of Mr. Lynch's cinema are *Blue Velvet* and now, *Mulholland Drive*. They are weird enough to make the overall feel exciting and new, while at the same time retaining enough of standard narrative structure to avoid the alienation of his *Eraserhead* or *Lost Highway*.

As I began watching the movie I thought to myself that Mr. Lynch explores the themes of innocence and experience in both *Blue* and *Drive*. That both movies are roughly in the mystery genre is another similarity. Perhaps, that both movies occur in places Mr. Lynch has inhabited makes these more personal than some of his other features. A fictional Lumberton substituting for Missoula in *Blue* and here a dreamy and nightmarish L.A.

David Lynch brings along what I have come to recognize as his bag of tricks for this new film. Haunting mechanical sounds, Roy Orbison's catalog, lovely and talented ingenues, arch veterans, bizarre close-ups, and the ability to instill chills all make their appearance at some point.

While much of the movie explores our reactions to a place and its events, I think the most exciting part of the viewing experience was the great performances given by Naomi Watts and Laura Elena Harring. These actresses made me care for them and because either one or both of them are in almost every scene it made the picture more bearable than some of the stiff performances that actresses under Mr. Lynch's direction have inflicted on us in the past. Take Laura Dern, please!

I guess I really haven't even delved into the plot at all. You must go see it for yourself, don't you think?

Letter from the Editor

Movin' On
Originally published December 17, 2002.

I thought I would post something new to this site before a full year turned over. I think I barely made it.

For those of you without the privilege of a personal relationship with yours truly, I have moved to Durham, North Carolina. Thus, we are no longer a Montana newsmagazine.

As much as I loved the give-and-take of the newsy bits, I must examine the reality that this site was a great form of therapy for me as I obtained a divorce. When the divorce was complete, I stopped writing so much.

The outlaws and renegades are still at large. Warden Martz remains in power and

Monsieur Racicot holds even more as the head of the Republican Party. Can I help but wonder that if he wasn't in power we wouldn't have had all these problems over all these years? Did that sentence even make sense? As always, you supply the attitude.

I'm no longer wedded to writing every weekday. I think my ex-wife got that desire in the settlement. Hopefully, I can get it together more than once a year because I really enjoy writing this.

Furthermore, I won't examine the news and scandals of North Carolina, at least initially. Maybe in next year's column. I simply don't know enough about the area and the *Herald-Sun* does a great job of uncovering the skeletons on its own. Montana should be so lucky to have such a dedicated home for investigative journalists.

I will probably turn my attention to a more personal arena. The arts and experiences I enjoy will be fair game.

Speaking of which, I have made the acquaintance of an artist who I am sure is destined for greatness. I am writing of the Sherri Wood half of the dainty duo.

I'll try to explicate more at a later time, preferably less than an anum from this diem. Until then, keep the faith.

Gannon's to the Right of Me

Reportage with a Twist
Originally published December 23, 2002.

A classic Montana joke is that the most beautiful sight in all of the state is Butte in your rearview mirror. Can you blame me if I cast a backwards glance?

For those of you without the proper knowledge of Butte, America, I can only recommend a quick view of their newspaper's website. In particular, an article about Butte emerging from its dark times. How low can you go?

Pardon me a quick aside. While researching this story I came across an article about Butte native and current Montana governor Judy Martz. Why wouldn't she give herself an "A", indeed?

However, the main focus of this article is a company that has called Butte its home for over a century. That would be Touch America formerly doing business with its former assets as the Montana Power Company.

Perhaps, it is their latest press release announcing the sale of their long-distance voice accounts. Although a wisecrack about deck chair placement on a certain oceangoing vessel comes to mind with regard to this latest gamble to get working capital to stay afloat.

Nay, could it be their desire to issue dividends to their preferred shareholders while posting another consecutive quarter of losses? That's part of it.

A further part is that it appears to this trained eye that they are soon to be the subject of a takeover attempt by Brad M. Kelley of Boca Grande, Florida. He is the chairman of Commonwealth Brands, a fine purveyor of cigarettes, including the Bull Durham brand. There's that Durham connection. Yeah! (Here's a website that has nothing to do with this story but it appears to be for a Scandinavian band named Bull Durham, "http://listen.to/bulldurham". And, they're wearing Christmas hats. Bonus!)

Mr. Kelley, on his own – not as chairman of Commonwealth – is purchasing a substantial stake in Touch America. He currently has over 10% of the common stock of Touch America. Granted, this is not what it once was. It currently trades in the range of $.33 and has a market cap of $34 million. His shares would be approximately valued at $3.7 million.

With a stock price in this sort of a basement the New York Stock Exchange threatens to delist the company, which they did in November. This can only mean shame and ignominy for the company and the concurrent likelihood that they may not be in the grave but they can see it from here.

Shall I connect the parts? After you. No, after you. Is it any coincidence that following Mr. Kelley's purchasing and what must be presumed to be the company's impending demise that the executives decide to issue one more stocking full of dividends to its preferred shareholders?

For those Pollyannaish enough to believe that corporate America does not have a soul as black as night, I might refer you to yet another article from *The Montana Standard*. (For those not wanting to click through, the article quotes a mutual fund manager as comparing previous payouts to company executives as unprecedented. I would have thought those guys would have seen it all after Enron, et al.) Special kudos to the *Standard* for their willingness to peer into the heart of darkness. Also, a finger wagging to the *Standard*. Their archive area was so difficult to use that I have to reference this next article from the *Missoulian*'s archives even though it originally appeared in the Standard with the byline of Janine Jobe. It is so delicious that I have to include an original paragraph.

> "I realize 'golden parachutes' are part of corporate America, but this is a highly unusual case," said McKittrick. "The issues around Touch America will be taught in our business schools for years to come. It will become a benchmark of how not to do it. I'm extremely troubled by it all."

Hallelujah, Judge Thomas McKittrick! Praise be, Janine Jobe. District Court Judge McKittrick is ruling on a shareholder lawsuit regarding those same payouts. The *Merriam Webster's Collegiate Dictionary* definition of which lists payoff as a synonym.

So, layoffs, the sale of assets, the disappearance of the corporate name, all cannot be far behind. Montana's own is soon to belong to a Boca Grande, Florida cigarette seller. Happy Holidays!

When We Miss Her

A Requiem
Originally published April 28, 2003.

It's not often that this scribbler is touched, readers' commentary to the contrary. I feel moved to compose this day by a tragic event touching my life in that strange way which happens on occasion.

I had the privilege to attend a reading by Amanda Davis last Monday at The Regulator Bookshop in Durham. It is just a few blocks from my house and they have an exceptional reading and lecture series. I saw Christopher Hitchens there this fall.

What brought me out of the house was a need for some cheap entertainment and the opportunity to meet women. What made me enjoy myself was the reading by Ms. Davis.

A Durham native and onetime employee of The Regulator, Ms. Davis was promoting her new novel, *Wonder When You'll Miss Me*. It was her first ever reading.

Although nervous and inexperienced, she knew she was among friends. That can make all the difference to a young author and she noted and appreciated the support given to her.

Before she began, I grabbed a copy of her book and started to read her opening paragraphs. Well thought out, sensitive, emotional, the book was better than my always present suspicions would grant it.

Her reading, although hampered by her lack of experience, was able to put the book and its story in a positive light. The, one must assume, somewhat autobiographical tale of a former fat girl haunted by herself and running away to join the circus, had moments of poignancy and truth.

Questions from the audience were fielded in a friendly manner. She mentioned that she had some ringers in attendance. It was quite a brief affair, allowing me to return home before the start of prime time.

She answered one question about the cover of the book. I cringed subtlely when someone asked about the design. I was expecting her to say she had no influence in the choosing. Instead, she had enlisted a friend to design it based on a photograph from a book about French circuses.

    As I said it was brief, so it turns out was her life. She died in a plane crash on Friday with her parents. They were flying to Salisbury in North Carolina with her father at the controls.

Ted's Montana's Shill

A Review
Originally published March 1, 2004.

As the self-appointed arbiter of all things Montana and some things Carolina I decided to write a little review of my recent trip to Ted's Montana Grill. Perhaps, I can change Mr. Turner's fortunes one way or another. I can't do any worse than Gerald Levin.

First off, the service was very good. Barely a moment after sitting down a gentleman was getting me a beer and some half sours (sliced sections of cucumbers in a vinegar and salt solution). Very delicious.

The next thing I know I am given a sample of bison pot roast and mashed potatoes. Again, they were delicious. I decided to order the french dip.

While waiting I noticed the paintings decorating the place. Some, illustrative pieces in the manner of Bierstadt. One particularly friendly server named Dennis told me they were after some paintings in Ted's private collection. Overall, they weren't great but neither were they completely embarassing. One even reminded me of my beloved Yellowstone.

The photos are another matter. There are a few black-and-white ones scattered around. The composition is flat, as well the printing is indistinct. He would have done better to get some John Smart's.

About this time my dinner was served. The dip was great and the fries were very tasty. In addition, they had a multitude of sauces within easy reach at the counter. The buffalo meat itself was the best I have ever had.

Taking a few more moments to look around I noticed that some of the fixtures do not exactly jibe. The lamp and tin ceiling, ceiling fans, railroad clock, wood bar and back bar, tiffany-style lamps, they didn't all seem to correspond.

One slightly annoying aspect is the music pumped in at that particular moment was from *Annie Get Your Gun* or some other Westery Broadway show. How about some Jimmy Buffett, Neil Young, Nicolette Larson, or even the Sons of the Pioneers? I think they could afford to be a little more eclectic in their music choices. Nobody would really want to listen to the popular music of the early 20th-century, the main decor theme.

Overall, I had a really good time but it was getting a little dicey as I was headed to the bathroom. The photos were annoying me with their poor quality. The show tunes were getting on my nerves when I entered the facility.

The bathroom was done up in fixtures and tile work reminiscent of the early 20th, my favorite period for bathroom design. Little white honeycomb tiles meeting up with a floor length urinal, paradise. The best was yet to be though, for when I went to wash my hands they had Boraxo in a dispenser for the hand soap. Ted, bet the farm, your Montana Grill is the real deal.

I'm planning to return some night to enjoy a little buffalo prime rib.

Over 80° of Bush Google's My Party

5th Anniversary Column - Yeah!
Originally published September 11, 2005.

Over 80° Day

I propose that Montana have its own distinctive state holiday. This one could be celebration of life in all of its fine and many forms. Simply put, the new holiday should be Over 80° Day.

This day would take place in any city or county, jurisdiction to be determined by the citizens themselves, when the temperature goes over 80° for the high of the day. The citizens would also nominate a consulting authority, in most cases it would probably be the National Weather Service. However, some folks might want to choose a local weather broadcaster or honored citizen.

This holiday would obviously not occur at the same time across the state. Some places would celebrate it in April, some in May, some even in June. You know, the places celebrating it in June would probably really need it.

What makes it fun is its utter unpredictability. All of a sudden, the night before a big test, a fearless prognosticator states that tomorrow will be Over 80° Day. Children and their parents hug each other as they plan to go to the river or into the woods the next day.

I think within time, traditions will emerge. People will prepare Over 80° Day baskets ahead of time. People will write Over 80° Day songs. People will play Over 80° Day games. And, woe betide the employer who won't give their workers the day off.

Faith-based Pantywaist

Here (second story from the bottom) at http://www.imdb.com/news/sb/2005-09-09/ and here (original article) at http://www.thenation.com/doc/20050919/blumenthal and both referencing this original offending FEMA document at http://www.fema.gov/news/newsrelease.fema?id=18473 are pieces of evidence that the Bush administration blatantly used hurricane Katrina as a convenient opportunity to pitch their faith-based initiative idea. I have my own personal experience of seeing Bush on the TV make a point of mentioning all the great work done by faith-based organizations in Katrina's wake. This, I felt, was unnecessary and distractingly opportunistic even for the Bush squad.

It is disheartening to think that our leader only gives a crap about scoring political points as people die and suffer. The above original article by Max Blumenthal shows that it was not just my imagination. Bush and company really did use Katrina for a little faith-based back-scratching.

Google's Losing It

I have my suspicions that Google is becoming less and less relevant. (In the interest of full disclosure, I use Google's AdSense and Search on this web site.) Just today I entered the search term "Ebert Roeper" [quotes not in the original] as I was trying to find when they are broadcasting in my area. It seems they switched channels and times. It's a hassle but I will adapt. Anyway, here are the results. It looks pretty good you say. Well, why don't we toddle over to Yahoo!

It takes until the 12th link on Google to get a *Chicago Sun-Times* link and that is for a review of *The Passion of the Christ* from February of 2004. Also, I'm not just writing this because I can't get any of my columns to come up in Google's Search results. I swear on Bush's faith-based bee-hind!

Happy 5th Anniversary to *The Outrider*.

Yes, it was five years ago on September 11, 2000 that *The Outrider* first hit the electrons. Yes, September 11th. I am getting ready to pop a beer as soon as I get this up on the web. One toast will have to be to curse the bombing bastards to hell and recommend their victims to heaven.

It has been quite a journey. Although, not without its calm points.

I wish I could write something profound to celebrate but really the best way to mark the occasion is in the method I used above. Just to write some damn thing that actually matters.

Potato Nasher

Art & Architectural Review
Originally published October 3, 2005.

When you spend $23 million for an art museum you expect something for your efforts. I think Mr. Raymond Nasher and Duke University can be rightly proud of their accomplishment in producing the new Nasher Museum of Art at Duke University.

While thinking that Rafael Viñoly's seemingly clunky five-appliances (It looks like you piled a refrigerator by a dishwasher by a washing machine by a clothes dryer by a trash compactor.) design is incongruous enough to detract from Duke's Gothic and Georgian splendor, I couldn't help but be moved by the natural and human elements retained in the building. The looming of the shop and office portion of the building as it towers over Duke University Drive is not unpleasant. Being a pedestrian as I surveyed the outer limits of the lot I felt as though I was seeing an imposing futuristic office building.

The entrances are well designed for walkers with sidewalks from Campus Drive and Anderson Street and there is even the sometimes neglected bicycle rack. Tooling around the outside, sidewalk only skirts so far, the interior atrium is inviting. With so many patrons in the building for the grand opening yesterday it felt a little bit like I was looking in on a piece of art itself. Then I realized, perhaps, the people inside felt something similar as they looked outside at me. The glass between the countertops gives the feeling of looking inside to a diorama or shadow box.

This impression that the interior of the building is neatly contained gives way to a glorious rushing of wonder at entering an incredible public space. At 13,000 square feet the vast courtyard with its Chinese inspired meshing support beams provided a stage and meeting place approaching the finest I have ever seen. I think you could read on people's faces that they were enjoying this exemplary feeling given by design.

Compared to the magnificence that is the Nasher, my complaints are truly minimal. The gift shop is almost woefully inadequate. It is hard to believe that a shop that small was designed in the 21st-century. Many museums have come to rely on their shops for substantial revenue. My guess is that they figured they didn't need the money.

However, there were some great blown glass kiwis in there that I lusted after. I didn't dare attempt to take them down. It was pretty crowded. It's small remember. Plus, they were on some pretty high shelves. Anyway, in no way do I have the money to buy a glass kiwi. If you have to ask us to bring it down off the shelf you can't afford it, you know.

Oh, here's another complaint. They were handing out bottled water but had no recycling containers for the empties. It is the law in Durham, after all. That's a small detail that was neglected although it really didn't diminish my enjoyment.

Finally, I thought one of the signs was kind of stupid. It was for the artwork called *Slate Line* I think. It said that oils from your hands can damage the artwork. I seriously doubt it. Why not just a simple sign saying "Don't Touch"? I guess that is not polite enough. Besides, they are simply stones set up like a path. Can they really be hurt that much?

So, enough bitchifaction, Raymond Nasher and Duke have done a truly splendiferous job of creating a modern major museum. This before I toured the galleries. It was way too crowded today and there were lines. I stepped into the theatre and watched *The Origins of the Night*, a glorious color film set in the Amazon with the natural sounds and lighting creating a mesmerising result.

In listening to Mr. Nasher on Thursday at the Carolina Theatre for the Mary and Jim Semans Lecture series, I found a lot to admire about the gentleman. He wrote a column while attending Duke in the '40's that Duke needed a new center for cultural offerings. Now, he has provided it.

He also proved frugal in his acquisition of sculpture as he said that he often found it priced at twenty times less that the price of comparably framed paintings by the same artists. Now the prices are nearing parity but not before Mr. Nasher got his bargains and shared them with us to my delight.

Strange Parallels

The Curious Case of Harriet Miers
Originally published October 26, 2005.

With apple-doll-faced Harriet Miers' impending confirmation/imolation I thought I would give a peep about crony Miers' strangely Gumplike coincidences.

Let me start by saying I think we should all give crone Miers the benefit of the doubt. She seems amply able to be a Supreme Court Justice. If it were not for two very significant issues in which she is on the opposite shore from this lecturer, I think she could be a good justice. So, have I made up my mind? Not yet, still.

In order of their appearance in the press, I will rattle down our two very significant points of contention. First up, *The Wall Street Journal* reported that decrepit Miers wanted the courts to dismiss the perfectly reasonable charge that (And you'll probably need a subscription, ya bum.) heart-attack-in-waiting Cheney was a Texan. This was to prevent the invocation of the 12th Amendment prohibition against a presidential and vice-presidential candidate from the same state counting that selfsame state's votes as their own. Once upon a time, this scribbler inveighed against fatboy Cheney for pretzeling himself to become an erstwhile Wyomingite.

While that episode displayed the disrespect this administration had for the constitution, fey Miers defense of this manipulation is, perhaps, illustrative of her thinking on constitutional issues. She asked that the justices deciding this matter use the "broad and inclusive" interpretation of the constitution. Yes, one that rat Cheney could drive a truck through.

So, to call her a constitutional liberal is accurate, at least, where Republicans and their homes are located. Well, the second matter happens to coincide with the tale of another Republican and her home. All the better that it is a story with resonance for old Miers and her pecuniary gain, as well as this electron smasher's previous digital meanderings.

Sunken-faced Miers' family received a very, very generous payment from Texas for land near an off-ramp needed for Superfund. Ta, *Billings Gazette*. Does this sound familiar to devoted readers of this column? Could it be that wrinkly Miers took a page from the playbook of our beloved Granny Martz?

For those who don't want to click through to all the hyperlinks, handout Martz herself gained immensely from land close to an off-ramp for which a company under her Superfund jurisdiction, Arco, accepted underpayment. What is it with Republicans and land near an off-ramp that also happens to be tremendously valuable when Superfund is involved?

Do meetings happen at the Republican Governors and Hangers-On Convention? Superfund Off-ramps and You: The Road to Wealth. Psst, Yo Miers, have I got a Superfund Off-ramp for you.

Anyway, haggish Miers seems to be very liberal when it comes to money her family is to receive for property she owns. All in all, I think we can be convinced that she is likely to be very generous when her financial or political interests are involved.

As mean as I am being to witchy Miers, I still think we should allow her to speak for herself and provide explanations. It is possible that I am just jumping the gun in thinking that she is a political hack.

Cats Carry Cary

Homesickness & Reunion
Originally published November 20, 2005.

Reading the Montanan which I once made them stop giving to me and which they started giving to me again anyway, I always thought it would be fun to attend one of the satellite Cat-Griz matchups put on across the country. This was before I even moved anywhere.

I figured the camaraderie and good times, being in the presence of other Montanans, even Cat fans, would have a salubrious effect no matter where I found myself. I was not far wrong. It's always good to engage in a little intra-state rivalry even being 2,000 miles from Montana.

Playing host for this 105th matchup (Take that you lesser but better known rivalries.) was Jaimie Marinkovich (Sorry if it's spelled wrong.) for the Griz and Duncan (Didn't catch your last name.) for the Cats at Woody's Sports Pub in Cary, North Carolina; Woody's, a place with a pretty decent beer selection and generally excellent service.

With a lack of bar fights, broken noses, hard feelings (I'm only speaking for myself.) and lost bets (I never saw anyone pay or any wagers being placed.) we had the pleasure of watching Travis Lulay and the Cats whomp up on the Griz in Bozeman. A city, whose surroundings never fail to astonish me in their beauty.

It is somewhat similar to a family where a squabble is always best left between brothers. In other words, if the Griz are going to lose to anyone, it hurts a little better when it is to a Montana State team.

Having written that, I can't help but say that the Griz stunk up the field and didn't really look like a championship caliber team. They were possibly not used to getting so muddy. Although, I did hear some grumblings from Griz fans that the Cats had made the field a little wetter than meteorological conditions would indicate.

However, you have to hand it to Travis Lulay. He looked great on the field. He was scrambling, passing, handing off, and just generally excellent. It is a shame he's not going to have a little postseason time to show off his stuff. But, Cats, you need to get it together in the regular season to see December.

One more slam on the Griz. I love you guys but could you make a tackle, please. The best Griz tackle I saw yesterday was at Woody's where a lady Griz fan grabbed a little Bobcat fan. She got him down!

A few words about Cary before I go. Cary, North Carolina is an intriguing mix of small town/huge bedroom community for Raleigh and Research Triangle Park. It does have an actual history and a train station (Whitefish to Cary anyone?) but there does seem to be a lack of there there. Local wags have dubbed Cary an acronym for "Containment Area for Relocated Yankees" (That would be us. Yes, Montanans are considered Yankees down here.) or "Can't Afford Raleigh Yet".

Notwithstanding it's lack of je ne sais quoi, Cary has a great independent movie theater in the Galaxy Cinema that serves samosas and shows Bollywood movies for the sizeable East Indian community. It also has incredible East Indian markets and ethnic delis. You'll know where to find me when Cat-Griz 106 rolls around.

Burns Misspeaks, Or Does He? Or Does He?

What the ???
Originally published January 17, 2006.

Lordy, Lordy, Look Who's Put Their Foot in It Again.

Anyway, if I can avoid a fatal embolism as I write this. Not from anger, mind you, but from such sheer excitement at the size of the scoop I am bringing you, dear readers. Although, now that I think of it, it is one small slip for Burns, one giant leap for *The Outrider*.

As I was putting together *Montana Headline News* this morning I came across a story from the *Bozeman Daily Chronicle* that described Senator Burns' Monday meeting with their editorial board. In this story Burns claimed that he could not recall ever meeting Abramoff. Never, ever. In fact, he is going so far as to have his staff check his records to see if he did.

This story got my brain to whirling. Didn't he say that he had met Abramoff once in an article last week? Well, checking the previous issues of *Montana Headline News* I came up with a broken link to the article in the *Helena Independent Record*. After a quick dip in their archives I pulled up this story wherein Burns claimed to have met Abramoff once. That story is dated January 10, 2006. So much for Burns' faulty memory.

With my head already in danger of blowin' up and my desire to write up this little incongruous piece of information from Burns I proceeded to produce Montana Headline News for all you good citizens out there anxiously awaiting the latest, greatest digest of Montana news. However, what should I come across but another story about Senator Burns.

In this *Missoulian* story Burns again says he met Abramoff once. Oh my Jehosophat! This was, like the *Bozeman Daily Chronicle* story, a Monday meeting with the editorial staff. The *IR* story last week was with the Lee Newspapers' State Bureau Reporters.

There you have it folks. Burns claimed in the January 10th *IR* story to have met Abramoff once. Then, in separate interviews on Martin Luther King Jr. Day, January 16th, he claimed to have both met Abramoff once and claimed to have never, ever met Abramoff.

I think my head swelling is starting to go down, now, that I got this out. Fortunately, I am not like one of those *Star Trek* computers that explode when confronted with two contradictory pieces of information. I am able to hold both of Senator Conrad Burns' stories in my mind simultaneously without injury to myself or others.

In other Senator Conrad Burns information, he seems to understand the importance of keeping quiet while involved in a lawsuit when he ignored Elouise Cobell, the lead plaintiff in the ongoing Interior Department trust fund suit, while she sat next to him on a plane. He apparently decided it was better to work on a crossword puzzle. Every word has its place on one of those. No two words will work for one space.

But, before I beat up on Senator Conrad Burns, and believe me I've been holding back, I thought we should leave him with the last words. In a bit of reportage for the *missoulian.com* Burns said, "I deal in truth. I don't deal in perceptions." Here, here, Senator Burns. Oops, forgot to wipe the sarcasm off that last part.

[Final section of story added on February 5, 2006] What is a guy to do? Senator Burns just said in this February 3rd interview with the *Daily Interlake* that, "I wouldn't know this Abramoff from a bale of hay," in claiming again that he never has met Abramoff. Is it any coincidence that Burns

claims to have met Abramoff with papers
from one chain while disclaiming any
meeting with two different papers?

Mirror, Mirror, On the Wall, Who's the Greatest 3-Point Shooter of Them All?

A Sports Story

Originally published February 15, 2006.

Every now and again, comes a story that manages to unite Montana and Durham. It is rare but it does happen. This is a great one.

As I was awakening this morning I heard on the radio that J.J. Redick from that little old university up the block set a new NCAA record for 3-point shots scored. On Tuesday versus Wake Forest he managed to boost his all-time record to 416. Amazing.

So, imagine my surprise (I don't follow sports that closely.) when I see that Cameron Muñoz of Montana State University - Billings was also a 3-point shooting star. In fact, he, too, has 416 3-pointers scored in his career.

He, too, is in the NCAA, albeit Division II.

Well, if this isn't a great little Sammy Sosa/Mark McQuire story (pre-steroid scandal, of course) or even a little Roger Maris/Mickey Mantle saga. Granted, the Yellowjackets are not up to the astonishing caliber of Duke, however, a 3-point shot is usually little defended and is primarily an example of pure, shooting prowess.

Although, the leagues are different, the game remains the same and the 3-pointer is the acid test of basketball accuracy from a distance. So, how do they stack up, J.J. is 6-foot-4 and Munoz is 6-foot-3 with a nation-leading 5.6 3-pointers a game (or, so says the Billings Gazette).

Wow, what more can I say? I don't think I could ever make it as a sportswriter. Well, here go a few thoughts.

That Durham thinks it is the center of the basketball universe and would not deign to consider a lower division's hot shooter. Yes.

That Cameron Munoz is not yet even the record holder as he still has to surpass the Division II record of 443. So does J.J.

That a little bit of thought about basketball records goes a long way. It do.

Montana Headline News... Brilliant Headlines

Book Bonus
Originally published as part of Montana Headline News 2005-2006

Death Cage Cat Pulled from Clark Fork Ice
Club Boxers are Punch Drunkards
Mid-Intersection Nap Nabs Safe Stealer
Unslaughterable Molly B. to Stay
Strange Godfellows
Brother, Sister in Downtown Beatdown
Cinema Shuffle Deals G.F. Out
Bitterroot Bill, Marmot, Says Spring
Libby Dam's $250m Sturgeon Turbine
Ranchers, Reccers Spar over Breaks
Bull Doctor Proctor Dispenses with Rider
Time: Burns is Last Worst Disgrace
Harlow. Squirt Gun Fight Turns Deadly
Lady Griz Golf Has Heart of Steele
Helena Writer Blasts Corpocracy
Gov to UM Grads: One Word...Energy
Cooking Club Seeks Economies of Scale
NIFL Team Big Sky Thunder Claps Shut
GOP Ad Questions Tester's Haircut
Tester's Barber Responds
Jobless Rate up, the Wage also Rises
Tester Pours Beer, Burns Tours Wine

Further Burns Firefighter Furor
Out-of-Biocontrol Flies Yield Jumbo Mice
Burns Boosts Bomb Bees Bill
Geocachin' Passion
Arlee School Field Trip Beer Lessons
Bozeman Doc, Everest Doc in New Doc

Montana Headline News... Headline Typos

Book Bonus
Originally published as part of Montana Headline News 2005-2006

Breast Dancer's 'Dirty Little Secret'
Governor Chides Ded Bison Approach

Montana Headline News... Funny Headlines

Book Bonus
Originally published as part of Montana Headline News 2005-2006

Officers in Sling for Erectile Drug Probe
'Cats Rip Their Sac State Rivals
Puma vs. Pussy vs. Power
Ancient Chinese Secret
Men Sought for Crotch Shots
Yo! Aggressive Urban Deer Here
Good Samaritan Sex Solicitation
Diaper Caper Fails at Dump Truck
Life's End Institute Dying
Hotter Nights Have Been in Montana
Icy Roads Drive People Glazy
Gardiner Teens' Missionary Efforts
Erectile Drug Probe Falls Hard on Officers
3,000 Panties & Child Porn Charges
Natural Gas Bills Expand
Tailpipe Recipes Won't Exhaust You
"What's Bears got to do with the Mine?"
Who Wants to be a Legislator?
Piano Mover Earns Laurels for Hardiness
Global Warming Riders Freeze
Can They Pull Off Duct Tape Dress?
Gasoline Prank Backfires

Sex Religion Passes Collection Plate
From Roadkill to Rhododendrons
Walk-Up Drive Through Robbery
Nude Photographer to Move to Butte
Vagina Monologues Engrossing
Hunter Safety Instructor Pulls a Cheney
Squeaky Krysko Looks Set to Get Grease
Sewellite Sewer Fight
Festival of the Dead Could Die
Bar Swamper: "It's the Level of Vomiting"
The Mill Levies of Madison County
Tester Says He's Bester
60-Foot Long Shortcake
Grounds for Coffee Burglary Charges
Podiatrist Caught in Sting Given Boot
Stones Fans Gettin' No Ticket Satisfaction
Arlee School Field Trip Beer Lessons

Montana Headline News... Funny Phrases

Book Bonus
Originally published as part of Montana Headline News 2005-2006

Artist John Maxwell Bear Tusk plays "Amazing Grace" on his Golden Eagle...

For many years after it happened, Robert Sallee never thought much...

The slogan seems to ring true: Whatever it is, you can get it on eBay, even Butte...

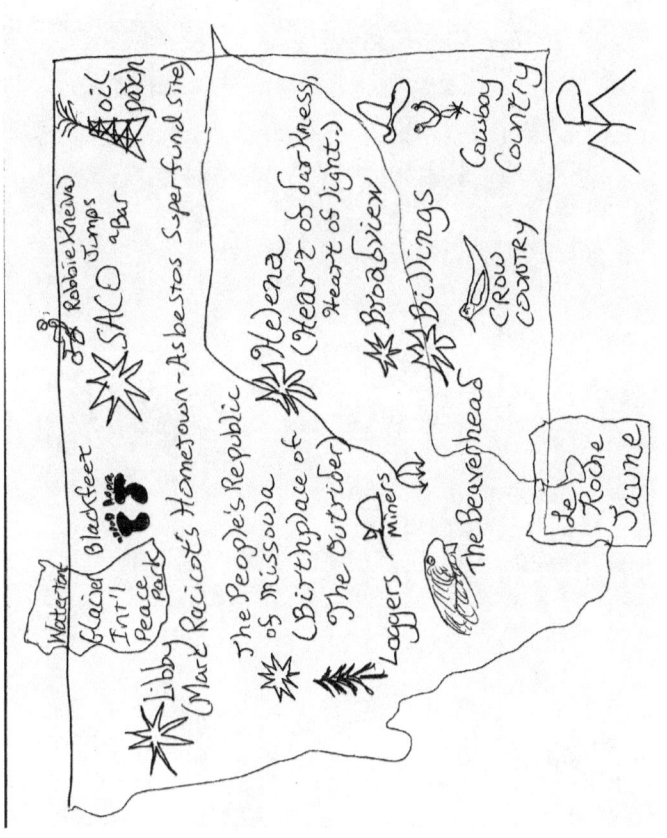

Other Works by the Author

Party Like a Lacrosse Star

Your Healthcare Sucks

Lies
(21st-Century Edition)

www.ingramcontent.com/pod-product-compliance
Lightning Source LLC
Chambersburg PA
CBHW021804220426
43662CB00006B/171